DISCOVERY GUIDE
# GOD HEARD THEIR CRY

## The Faith Lessons™ Series
## with Ray Vander Laan

DISCOVERY GUIDE
# GOD HEARD THEIR CRY

THAT THE WORLD MAY KNOW®

5 FAITH LESSONS BY
## RAY VANDER LAAN
**with Stephen & Amanda Sorenson**

ZONDERVAN®        FOCUS ON THE FAMILY.

ZONDERVAN.com/
AUTHORTRACKER
*follow your favorite authors*

ZONDERVAN

*God Heard Their Cry Discovery Guide*
Copyright © 2009 by Ray Vander Laan

Requests for information should be addressed to:

Zondervan, *Grand Rapids, Michigan 49530*

Focus on the Family and the accompanying logo and design are federally registered trademarks of Focus on the Family, *Colorado Springs, Colorado 80995.*

That the World May Know and Faith Lessons are trademarks of Focus on the Family.

ISBN 978-0310-29121-3

All maps are courtesy of International Mapping.

Photos on pages 39, 44, 62, 78, 86, and 134 are courtesy of Ray Vander Laan. All other photos are courtesy of Mark Tanis.

All illustrations are courtesy of Rob Perry.

*Interior design by Ben Fetterley*

*Printed in the United States of America*

10 11 12 13 14 15 • 25 24 23 22 21 20 19 18 17 16 15 14 13 12 11 10 9 8 7 6 5 4 3 2

# CONTENTS

# INTRODUCTION

"Let my people go!"

With these simple words, spoken more than 3,200 years ago (Exodus 5:1), God sent Moses to confront the most powerful ruler on earth. By these words, the God of the universe revealed that he had heard the cry of his suffering people. Deeply moved, he revealed himself as the God of love and mercy. He acted with awesome power to deliver the Hebrews and establish them as his chosen instrument to reveal himself to the world.

Few words recorded in the Hebrew Bible, or anywhere for that matter, are more familiar to people today than the words, "Let my people go!" And few events are more central to the stories of both the Hebrew text (Old Testament) and the Christian text (New Testament) than the great redemptive acts of God and the people of the exodus. The Hebrew text refers to the exodus theme more than 120 times, plus there are multiple references to related concepts such as manna, water from the rock, Mount Sinai, and the Ten Commandments. The Christian text mentions Moses eighty-five times and Egypt twenty-nine times.

Yet there is more to the exodus than first meets the eye. The historical account is most useful in understanding God and his desire for the Hebrews to become his witnesses to the world. It is central to understanding why many followers of Jesus considered him to be the prophet like Moses — the Messiah — whom the Lord had promised to send (Deuteronomy 18:17 – 19; Luke 7:16; 24:19 – 20; John 6:14). Jesus often used ideas found in the exodus story, and many of his teachings interpret Moses' words in the Torah. Jesus also positioned his redemptive acts against the background of festivals — Passover, Unleavened Bread, and First Fruits — that are associated with the Hebrews' deliverance from Egypt.[1] And at the deepest level, the exodus story not only provides a background for God's plan to bring Jesus into the world as Messiah, it is one of the first chapters in God's great redemptive story to restore shalom — unity, harmony, order — to his broken creation.

Genesis, the first book of the Torah, provides the necessary background for the exodus. Genesis describes God creating a perfect, harmonious universe out of chaos and then describes how sin destroyed that universe, resulting in the loss of harmony in God's creation and the return of chaos. In the stories of the exodus we find the very foundations of the restoration of shalom to God's world. Future characters in the Scriptures, including Jesus, build on that foundation. To study these amazing events is to discover that there is really one story — the story of God's redemption. Despite the many failures of God's people in fulfilling their role in that story, God's power has and continues to flow through his flawed human instruments (Jesus excepted, of course) to bring to fruition his plan of redemption.

"Let my people go" was the cry of the Hebrews in Egypt. In a sense, it is also the cry of anyone who has recognized the bondage of sin and the destruction it produces. Thus the exodus is a paradigm for our own experience, and we Christians describe our deliverance in similar language because God delivers us by his mercy and the protecting blood of the Lamb — Jesus Christ. Without the exodus, we would not be who we are — redeemed people delivered by the God of Israel. In that sense, the victory of the ancient Hebrews must become our victory. We, like the ancient Hebrews whom God delivered from the hand of Pharaoh, must stand in awe and declare that our God is King.

## Clarifying Our Terminology

In this study, the record of God's reclaiming and restoring his broken world is called the Bible, Scripture, or the "text." Having studied in the Jewish world, I believe it is important to communicate clearly how the nature of that inspired book is understood. Although it can be helpful to speak of Scripture in terms of Old and New Testaments, these descriptions also can be misleading if they are interpreted to mean old and outdated in contrast to a new replacement. Nothing, in my opinion, is further from the truth. Whereas the

"New Testament" describes the great advance of God's plan with the arrival of the Messiah and the promise of his completed and continuing work, the "Old Testament" describes the foundational events and people through whom God began that work. The Bible is not complete without both testaments; it comprises God's one revelation, his one plan to reclaim his world and restore harmony between himself and humankind. To emphasize that unity, I prefer to refer to the Hebrew text (Old Testament) and the Christian text (New Testament) that together are the inspired, infallible Word of God.

The language of the Bible is bound by culture and time. The geography of the lands of the Bible — Egypt, the desert, the Promised Land — shaped the people who lived there, and biblical writers assumed that their readers were familiar with the culture of that world. Many Christians today, however, lack even a basic geographical knowledge of the region and know even less of the ancient cultures that flourished there. So understanding the Scriptures involves more than knowing what the words mean. It also means becoming familiar with the everyday experiences and images the text employs to reveal God's message so that we can begin to understand it from the perspective of the people to whom it originally was given.

For example, the ancient Hebrew people to whom God revealed himself described their world in concrete terms. Their language was one of pictures, metaphors, and examples rather than ideas, definitions, and abstractions. Whereas we might describe God as omniscient or omnipresent (knowing everything and present everywhere), they would describe him as "my Shepherd." Thus the Bible is filled with concrete images from Hebrew culture: God is our Father and we are his children, God is the Potter and we are the clay, Jesus is the Lamb killed on Passover, heaven is an oasis in the desert, and hell is the city sewage dump.

Many of the Bible's images occur first during the exodus: Israel as God's bride, God as shepherd, the desert as a metaphor for life's difficult experiences, God as living water, God as king, God carrying his people on eagle's wings, the saving blood of the lamb. The Hebrews experienced these and many more familiar images as they left Egypt, spent forty years in the desert, and then entered the Promised Land.

The text frequently describes the people themselves, the descendants of Abraham, as "Hebrews," which probably originated from the Egyptian *habiru* meaning "dusty ones" (a reference to their desert origins). Genesis refers to Abraham as "the Hebrew" (Genesis 14:13), and after God gave Jacob the name *Israel*, the text also calls his descendants *Israelites*. The term *Jew* is not used until much later in history (see the books of Nehemiah and Esther). We will generally use the word *Hebrew* because that is how the people were known in the land of Egypt.

The Hebrew text refers to the land God promised to Abraham as *Canaan* or *Israel*. The Christian text calls it *Judea*. After the Second Jewish Revolt (AD 132 – 135), it was known as *Palestine*. Each of these names resulted from historical events that took place in the land at the time the terms were coined.

One of the earliest designations of the Promised Land, *Canaan,* probably meant "purple," referring to the dye produced from the shells of murex shellfish along the coast of Phoenicia. In the ancient world, this famous dye was used to color garments worn by royalty, and the word for the color referred to the people who produced the dye and purple cloth. Hence, in the Bible, *Canaanite* refers to a "trader" or "merchant" (Zechariah 14:21), as well as to a person from the "land of purple," or Canaan.

*Israel*, another designation for the Promised Land, derives from the patriarch Jacob. His descendants were known as the Hebrews as well as the children of Israel. After they conquered Canaan during the time of Joshua, the name of the people, *Israel,* became the designation for the land itself (in the same way it had with the Canaanites). When the nation split following the death of Solomon, the name Israel was applied to the northern kingdom and its territory, while the southern land was called Judah. After the fall of the northern kingdom to the Assyrians in 722 BC, the entire land was again called Israel.

During the time of Jesus, the land that had been the nation of Judah was called *Judea* (which means "Jewish"). Because of the influence the people of Judea had over the rest of the land, the land itself was called Judea. The Romans divided the land into several provinces: Judea, Samaria, and Galilee (the three main divisions during Jesus' time); Gaulanitis, the Decapolis, and Perea (east of the Jordan River);

and Idumaea (Edom) and Nabatea (in the south). Later during the Roman era (about one hundred years after Jesus' death), the land was called *Palestine*. Although the Egyptians had referred to the land where the Philistines lived as *Palestine* long before Roman times, the Roman emperor Hadrian popularized the term as part of his campaign to eliminate Jewish influence in the area.

Today the names *Israel* and *Palestine* are often used to designate the land God gave to Abraham. Both terms are politically charged. *Palestine* is used by Arabs living in the central part of the country, and *Israel* is used by Jews to indicate the political State of Israel. In this study, *Israel* is used in the biblical sense. This does not indicate a political statement regarding the current struggle in the Middle East, but best reflects the biblical designation for the land.

Present-day Egypt is a beautiful and advanced country, and we do not identify the "Egyptians" of the Bible as identical to the Egyptians of today any more than we would think of the present prime minister of Egypt as the descendant of the Pharaohs. Nor do we draw any political conclusions regarding relationships between the modern state of Israel and the country of Egypt. Throughout the production of this study, we were warmly welcomed and treated with great hospitality in both countries. Our goal is to study God's work with his Hebrew people as he freed them from slavery in ancient Egypt.

## Establishing the Historic and Geographic Setting

When studying the exodus of the Hebrews from Egypt, it is natural to ask, "When did that event occur?" Or, to ask it another way, "Who was the Pharaoh 'who did not know about Joseph'?" (Exodus 1:8). There are two basic theories.[2] One places the biblical event in the eighteenth Egyptian dynasty around 1450 BC, during the reign of Pharaohs such as Thutmose (3) or Amenhotep (2).[3] The other places it in the nineteenth dynasty, during the reign of Ramses the Great (1213 – 1279 BC).[4] Significant textual and scientific support exists for each perspective.

Although I have my opinion on the matter, this study does not attempt in any way to argue for one position or the other. The foundational position for this study is that the exodus occurred as the Bible describes it. Since the Bible does not name the Pharaoh (a word similar to *king* in English), God apparently did not believe this fact to be central to his message. However, in much the same way that one studies ancient languages or uses a good commentary, it is helpful to study specific cultural settings in order to better understand the biblical text. Thus this study focuses on Pharaoh Ramses the Great, not because he was the Pharaoh of the exodus but because he is the epitome of all Pharaohs. Whoever the Pharaoh of the exodus was, we can be sure he wanted and tried to become like Ramses the Great. By focusing our efforts in this way, we will gain a sense of the culture of the time of the exodus (the two theories are relatively close in time anyway) without the burden of the controversy regarding specific dates.

I hold a similar position regarding the route of the exodus. There are many proposed routes and this study does not seek to support one over another. Rather, I have chosen for this study the type of terrain and culture that would represent whichever route the Hebrews took. If knowing the support for the varying points of view is important to you, other studies should be consulted.

## God Reclaims His World through History

From the beginning, God planned to reclaim his world from the chaos of sin. He revealed his plan to restore shalom to his creation to Noah, Abraham, Isaac, Jacob, and their families. The books of the Torah, which tell the creation and exodus stories, revealed to the Hebrews who God is, who they were, and who they needed to become. Thus the Torah is God's blueprint describing the role he desires his people to play in his plan of restoration. It forms the foundation of all future acts of God recorded throughout the Bible.

The Hebrews were to be witnesses of God's plan to reclaim his world. Their interaction with the Egyptians and their king, Pharaoh, certainly revealed the nature of the creator of the universe and his desire for his creation (Exodus 8:10; 9:13 – 14). After they reclaimed the Promised Land, the descendants of the Hebrews made God known to many nations as people from all over the world traveled through Israel.

Although his people often have failed in their mission to live righteously and reveal the one true God — *Yahweh*, God continues to use humans as instruments of his redemption. The mission of God's people today is the same one he gave to the ancient Hebrews and Israelites: to live obediently *within* the world so that through us *the world may know that our God is the one true God.* Living by faith is not a vague, otherworldly experience; rather, it is being faithful to God in whatever place and time he has put us.

The message of the Scriptures is eternal and unchanging, and the mission of God's people remains the same, but the circumstances of the people of the Bible are unique to their times. Consequently, we most clearly understand God's truth when we know the cultural context within which he spoke and acted and the perception of the people with whom he communicated. This does not mean that God's revelation is unclear if we don't know the cultural context. Rather, by cultivating our understanding of the world in which God's story was told, we will begin to see it as an actual place with real people and a real culture.

As we explore the Egypt of the Bible and study the people and events in their geographic and historic contexts, we will discover the *who*, *what*, and *where* of the exodus story and will better understand the *why*. By learning how to think and approach life as Amram, Jochebed, Moses, Aaron, Miriam, Joshua, Phineas, and other Hebrews, we will discover that we too experience "Egypt" in our lives. And, like the ancient Hebrews, we will discover that it is much easier for God to get us out of Egypt than to get Egypt out of us.

The intent of this study is to enter the world of the Hebrews and familiarize ourselves with their culture and the cultures of their day so that we may fully apply the Bible's message to our lives. We will seek to better understand God's revealed mission for the events and characters of the exodus from Egypt and the forty years of training (testing) in the desert so that we, in turn, will better understand God's purpose in Jesus' life and in our lives. Our purpose is to follow God's intent as revealed to Ezekiel:

Son of man, look with your eyes and hear with your ears and pay attention to everything I am going to show you, for that is why you have been brought here. Tell the house of Israel everything you see.

                                                          Ezekiel 40:4

"Let my people go!"

These words still ring with power and clarity after more than 3,000 years. God still seeks to free his people and his world from the chaos that sin has brought to it. Now he invites you, as he invited Israel, the Egyptians, and even Pharaoh, to experience the freedom to serve and worship (in Hebrew, both words are the same!) him as the one, true God.

# HOW BIG IS OUR GOD?

God loves a story. In fact, one could describe the Bible as one story made up of many stories. Yet when we read the Bible, we tend to concentrate on the individual stories without considering how each story fits into and contributes to the greater story that God is unfolding. This is particularly true of the story of the exodus of the Hebrew slaves from Egypt. God's protective care for his chosen people thrills us. His demonstrations of power through the plagues and the dividing of the Red Sea amaze us. Yet we seldom consider God's greater story of which the exodus is but an early chapter. So let's begin by discovering where the story of the exodus fits into that greater story.

God's greater story began when he created the universe out of a watery chaos (which he also had created). God's creation culminated in his formation of two humans, Adam and Eve, who were to partner with him in caring for his world. However, they rebelled against the terms of their partnership with God and reintroduced chaos to the harmony of God's creation.

Fortunately, God's story did not end with the return of chaos. Instead, he began a long process of restoring harmony (the Bible calls it *shalom*) to his creation. What is truly amazing is that he chose to accomplish this process in partnership with people — the same created beings who had ruined it in the first place! He commands his created human beings to live lives that bring harmony to his creation and forbids whatever causes brokenness or prevents the restoration he desires. Into this story he invites the Hebrews, the descendants of the patriarchs, to partner with him so that through them the whole world will know of God's restoration of shalom.

But God's story is not the only story. The other story can be traced to the evil one, the snake, the deceiver who tempted Adam and Eve. He loves chaos and seeks to destroy the shalom of God's creation. The evil one promises harmony and the defeat of the chaos that causes pain, but his definition of harmony actually creates the very brokenness from which he promises deliverance. By the time of the exodus, that story had become the story of all cultures, including the culture of Egypt. That is why the story written in the stones of Egypt is so important. The spectacular temples, architectural details, and carvings in stone found in ancient Egypt are, in effect, the sacred text of that other story.

God's plan required a confrontation between these two stories (or worldviews as some would label them). People need to know the truth about chaos and the shalom, or restoration, that God promises. People need to understand that the way of this world is a lie that only increases the brokenness that permeates life. Perhaps that is why Jacob and his descendants found themselves in Egypt, where they saw and experienced the stark contrast between the two stories. If they were to be God's partners in defeating the lie and restoring shalom to God's creation, they needed to know both stories and commit themselves to living out his story in his way.

So while the fact of the Hebrews' miraculous delivery from slavery in Egypt is a dramatic historical event, it is much more than that. The presence of the Hebrew slaves within the culture of the great empire of ancient Egypt brings into focus the cosmic conflict between the stories of chaos and shalom. As part of his unfolding story of the restoration of shalom to his broken creation, it is no wonder that God used a great and mighty demonstration of his power over chaos to deliver the Hebrew slaves from Egypt.

The experiences of God's people in the exodus are not only the first chapter of God's great story of restoration but are a metaphor, a paradigm, of that restoration as well. God's plan of restoration for his people (or salvation as it is sometimes called) is rooted in the exodus and built on the exodus experiences. The two stories — God's restoration of shalom versus the chaos of the evil one — are present at all times and in all places, including our own. Thus the most important question for us is the same one both the Hebrews and the Egyptians had to answer: "If you understand the stories, whose story will you believe and live by?"

## Opening Thoughts (3 minutes)

### *The Very Words of God*

> *In the beginning God created the heavens and the earth. Now the earth was formless and empty, darkness was over the surface of the deep, and the Spirit of God was hovering over the waters.*
>
> *And God said, "Let there be light," and there was light. God saw that the light was good, and he separated the light from the darkness. God called the light "day," and the darkness he called "night." And there was evening, and there was morning — the first day.*
>
> *And God said, "Let there be an expanse between the waters to separate water from water." So God made the expanse and separated the water under the expanse from the water above it. And it was so. God called the expanse "sky." And there was evening, and there was morning — the second day.*
>
> *And God said, "Let the water under the sky be gathered to one place, and let dry ground appear." And it was so. God called the dry ground "land," and the gathered waters he called "seas." And God saw that it was good.*

*Genesis 1:1 – 10*

### Think About It

The structures people create and build — museums, bridges, tombs, government buildings, churches, performing arts centers, stadiums — say something about the people who built them and what those people value.

Consider some of the extraordinary structures people of our day build, such as the towering skyscrapers of Dubai, the Sydney Opera House, the "Bird's Nest" stadium built for the Olympics in Beijing. In what ways do these structures tell the "story" of our world? What do they reveal about who we are and how we believe the world works?

## DVD Notes (35 minutes)

The story of Egypt in stone—pyramids, temples, and architecture

God's story in the hearts of people—creation, chaos, and shalom

The temple of Amun Re—a theology of chaos and order

**The job of Pharaoh: to maintain Ma'at**

**Each story has a price tag**

# DVD Discussion (5 minutes)

1. The pyramids, temples, and gigantic stone carvings of ancient Egypt are truly amazing, but to realize that every detail — from the design and shape of the structures to the placement of Pharaoh's name in a cartouche — reveals something of the sacred story of the Egyptian culture is astounding. What did you learn about the Egyptian story that helps you to better understand what was at stake in the intersection of God's story and the Egyptian story in the exodus?

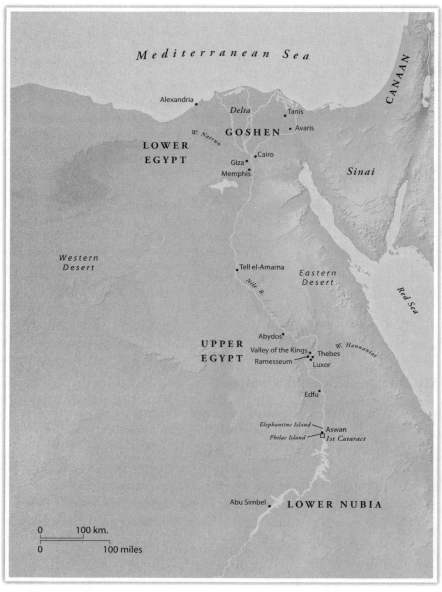

**THE ANCIENT EGYPTIAN STORY WAS SCULPTED AND ETCHED IN STONE THROUGHOUT THE EGYPTIAN EMPIRE. IT WAS WRITTEN IN THE GREAT STATUES AND TEMPLES OF ABU SIMBEL AT THE SOUTHERN END OF EGYPT, IN THE TEMPLES AND TOMBS OF KARNAK (THEBES), IN THE GREAT PYRAMIDS OF GIZA, IN THE ANCIENT CAPITAL CITY OF AVARIS (RA'AMSES), AND IN SCATTERED MINING SITES IN THE WILDERNESS DESERTS OF THE SINAI PENINSULA.**

2. According to the Egyptian story, why was it essential for Pharaoh to be responsible for all of the religious ritual in Egypt?

   What would be the consequences in daily life for all Egyptians if he failed?

3. What insights have you gained into the role that the story of a culture plays in shaping who people are and how they live?

   What have you realized about the cost of joining a culture's story?

   What might you gain by reexamining the importance of God's creation story to your beliefs and daily life?

# Small Group Bible Discovery and Discussion (11 minutes)

## Ma'at from Chaos — the Egyptian Story

Most of us are familiar with God's story of creation as told in the Bible, but Egypt had a creation story too. We can still read the "sacred text" of Egypt's story in the structure and carvings of its ancient temples. Like God's story, the Egyptian story tells about the establishment of order from chaos followed by the breakdown of that order and the resulting pain and suffering of life. But the Egyptian story has a different solution. It declares that chaos can be defeated by their gods and their ruler, Pharaoh, who was viewed as divine and brought harmony and order — called *ma'at* — to their world.

1. We may not expect to discover similarities between God's creation story and the Egyptian story, but it really should not surprise us when we do. The Egyptians experienced in their lives the same brokenness of sin — failed relationships, famine, violence, immorality — that we experience in ours, and their story certainly reflects a longing for order. What would be the source of their awareness of and longing for God's shalom? (See Psalm 19:1 – 4; 97:6; Acts 14:17; Romans 1:18 – 20.)

2. In a sense, the creation story in Genesis can be viewed as part of a preamble to the exodus story. So we might ask, why did Moses write it in the manner in which he did? Perhaps we can discover at least part of the answer by reading Genesis 1 – 2 and comparing God's creation story to the Egyptian creation story (see Profile of a Culture: Egypt's Creation

Story below). As you read, take note of and discuss the similarities and differences between the two stories and why they are significant.

| Genesis Account | Similarities to Egyptian Story | Differences from Egyptian Story |
|---|---|---|
| Gen. 1:1–10 | | |
| Gen. 1:11–25 | | |
| Gen. 1:26–2:3 | | |
| Gen. 2:4–17 | | |
| Gen. 2:18–23 | | |

## PROFILE OF A CULTURE
### Egypt's Creation Story

The Egyptian culture was a blend of several civilizations, so its religious traditions were actually a composite of several mythologies. It is not surprising, then, that there is some overlap and diversity in Egypt's creation story. Depending upon the era of Egyptian culture and the location, one god or another may be viewed as the supreme creator god.

Atum, for example, was the primeval god of Heliopolis, but in Thebes during the Middle and New Kingdom periods Amun Re (pronounced Ra) was the favored creator god. In Memphis, Ptah, one of Egypt's oldest gods, was revered as the sculptor of the earth and humans. This is why some accounts

*continued on next page . . .*

name one god as the creator while others name another god who seemingly does the same thing. Although these blended stories may be confusing or seem contradictory to Western thinkers, ancient Egyptians had little discomfort with these differences. So, in general, what follows is one rendering of Egypt's creation story:

Atum, the great creator god, stood on a mound that rose out of the watery, primordial swamp and spoke creation into existence. He created a space, like an air bubble, in the chaos of the cosmic ocean. He made the waters above the sky, and the waters below the earth. Between the sky and the earth he established the space where all life exists. So Atum brought order out of chaos.

Atum was considered to be the "self-engendered one" who arose at the beginning of time to create the world and the other gods (the gods of life and nature such as the sun, earth, sky, fertility, justice, the afterlife). As the father of Egypt's gods, he created these gods from his spit. The ram-headed god Khnum is also said to have used silt taken from the Nile to form a person on his potter's wheel. The goddess Heket then gave the breath of life to the clay figure.

3.  Try to imagine what it would be like if you had spent your life surrounded by representations of the Egyptian creation story and were hearing or reading the Genesis creation account for the first time.

    What might be familiar to you?

    What questions would you have, and what else would you want to know?

How might this new story change your perspective on what brings harmony and order to life?

4. In what ways does it make sense to you that Moses included the details he did in writing God's creation story for the Hebrews?

## Faith Lesson (5 minutes)

The Egyptian story, written in the stone of ancient Egypt, presented a worldview — a picture of what was most important in life and how life was supposed to work. That story matters because it was powerful. It shaped who people were and how they lived. And it came at a price. The focus of life according to the Egyptian story was to preserve ma'at — to maintain the harmonious order of the system — and to do so at *any* cost.

God's story presents a worldview too. In that story, there is one creator who is God, and he wants people who will join with him in restoring shalom to the chaos that results when people live according to the wrong story. But in order to join him, we have to know both stories. We then have to buy into God's story with all our heart, all our soul, and all our strength (Deuteronomy 6:4 - 5).

1. To what extent do you think the creation story, the religion, and the gods of Egypt affected the Hebrews' worldview and shaped who they were?

What evidence do you see that indicates they were being shaped by Egypt's story?

---

**DID YOU KNOW?**

Beginning with the exodus, and for generations thereafter, God repeatedly identified himself to Israel by saying, "I am the LORD your God." While that statement might seem obvious from our perspective today, Ezekiel 20:7 gives us a hint as to why God expressed his identity so emphatically: "Each of you, get rid of the vile images you have set your eyes on, and do not defile yourselves with the idols of Egypt."

Had the Hebrews actually bought into the Egyptian story to the point that they worshiped the gods of Egypt? It would certainly appear that that was the case. Joshua 24:14–24 makes it clear that the Israelites must choose between the two stories: "Throw away the gods your forefathers worshiped beyond the River and in Egypt, and serve the LORD" (v. 14).

---

2. How would you (briefly) describe the "story" of your culture?

3. To what extent has your culture's story and its "gods" affected your worldview and shaped who you are?

What in your life indicates that you are being shaped by that story?

What do you find in the opening chapters of God's story in Genesis that compels you to grab onto his story with all your heart, soul, and strength?

## Closing (1 minute)

Read together Deuteronomy 6:4–9: "Hear, O Israel: The Lᴏʀᴅ our God, the Lᴏʀᴅ is one. Love the Lᴏʀᴅ your God with all your heart and with all your soul and with all your strength. These commandments that I give you today are to be upon your hearts. Impress them on your children. Talk about them when you sit at home and when you walk along the road, when you lie down and when you get up. Tie them as symbols on your hands and bind them on your foreheads. Write them on the doorframes of your houses and on your gates."

Spend time in prayer, asking God to help you remember that the story we believe in and live by matters. Ask for his wisdom in recognizing the story of the evil one wherever it appears in our culture and for the strength to live according to God's story each day. Thank him for the invitation to join in his unfolding story and for the privilege of living and working in partnership with him to defeat the chaos of sin, thus restoring shalom to his creation.

## Memorize

*Hear, O Israel: The LORD our God, the LORD is one. Love the LORD your God with all your heart and with all your soul and with all your strength. These commandments that I give you today are to be upon your hearts. Impress them on your children. Talk about them when you sit at home and when you walk along the road, when you lie down and when you get up. Tie them as symbols on your hands and bind them on your foreheads. Write them on the doorframes of your houses and on your gates.*

*Deuteronomy 6:4 – 9*

# Choosing God's Story

*In-Depth Personal Study Sessions*

## **Day One** | God Demonstrates His Power over Chaos

### The Very Words of God

> On that day I swore to them that I would bring them out of Egypt into
> a land I had searched out for them, a land flowing with milk and
> honey, the most beautiful of all lands. And I said to them, "Each of you,
> get rid of the vile images you have set your eyes on, and do not defile
> yourselves with the idols of Egypt. I am the LORD your God."

*Ezekiel 20:6 – 7*

### Bible Discovery

### *God's Plan to Restore Shalom*

In a sense, the exodus experience is a paradigm for God's
ongoing work to exert his power over chaos and restore shalom
to his broken creation. Since creation itself is a demonstration of
God's power over chaos, it is not surprising to find parallel experiences in God's creation story and the exodus story. Perhaps that is
why Genesis, or *Bereshit* to the Hebrews, is the first book of the
Torah. It not only provides a counter-perspective to the Egyptian
story, it provides the background the Hebrews needed to understand their own story: who God was, who they were, and what
God was doing in his world. It also helps convey the idea that
through the exodus God is beginning something new in his plan
to restore his shalom.

1. At the beginning of creation (Genesis 1:1 – 10), God's Spirit
   (Hebrew, *ruach,* which also means "wind") hovered over
   the waters of chaos and separated them to create the land,
   sky, and seas. How did God, in a sense, repeat this conquest

of chaos at the beginning of the exodus, and what was the result? (See Exodus 14:21 – 22).

2.  When God decided to deliver his creation from the oppression of sin during the time of Noah (Genesis 6:5 – 18; 7:22 – 23), what did God use to save Noah and his family?

What did God use to save Moses, who in turn would save Israel from the oppression of sin in the land of Egypt? (See Exodus 2:1 – 3.)

NOTE: These are the only two places in the Hebrew text that the word, *tevah*, meaning "ark," is used.

3.  After the flood, the three sons of Noah and their sons became the fathers of the nations (seventy in all) and spread out over the earth (Genesis 10:1 – 32).

    a.  By the time Jacob went to Egypt to reunite with Joseph, how large was his family? (See Genesis 46:26 – 27; Exodus 1:1 – 5.)

    b.   What had happened to the descendants of Jacob during their time in Egypt? (See Exodus 1:6 – 7; Deuteronomy 10:22.)

    c.   How many heads of families (elders) were in Israel at the time of the Exodus? (See Exodus 24:1.)

4.   In God's creation story (Genesis 1:1 – 31), he commanded order out of chaos ten times: light from darkness, the formation of sky, land, seas, vegetation, lights — sun, moon, stars — in the the sky, creatures in the water, birds in the sky, living creatures on land, and man in his image. In contrast, what does God do to his creation through the ten plagues he inflicted on Egypt? (See Exodus 7:14 – 11:8.)

What does the contrast between God as Creator who made harmony out of chaos and then made chaos out of harmony reveal to us about God's relationship to his creation?

5.   In Exodus 20:8 – 11, God connects rest on the Sabbath to his creation. In Deuteronomy 5:12 – 15, to what is the Sabbath rest connected, and what do you think this meant to the Hebrews?

## Reflection

To the Hebrews at the time of the exodus, a pattern of parallel stories or repeated images such as the examples cited in the Bible Discovery section communicated something significant. They naturally
would have drawn a connection between what God was doing with
them through their experience in the exodus and what God was
doing when he created the world. For a moment, put yourself in the
Hebrews' shoes. Consider how you might think about your exodus
experience as being connected with, and a continuation of, the bigger story of all that God had been doing since he created the world.

How would this realization affect your thoughts about and commitment to God?

How differently might you view the importance (and the
impact) of your decisions and actions if you realized that what
was happening in your life was part of God's story, part of how
he planned to restore shalom to all things?

How much more important would your experience of the exodus be to you if you viewed it as a paradigm of God's work in the
world, much like his work in creation?

In what ways might the exodus reshape your view of yourself — your identity as one of God's people?

## Memorize

> *Ask now about the former days, long before your time, from the day God created man on the earth; ask from one end of the heavens to the other. Has anything so great as this ever happened, or has anything like it ever been heard of?... You were shown these things so that you might know that the LORD is God; besides him there is no other.*

> *Deuteronomy 4:32, 35*

# **Day Two** | The Return of Chaos

## The Very Words of God

> *During that long period, the king of Egypt died. The Israelites groaned in their slavery and cried out, and their cry for help because of their slavery went up to God. God heard their groaning and he remembered his covenant with Abraham, with Isaac and with Jacob. So God looked on the Israelites and was concerned about them.*

> *Exodus 2:23 – 25*

## Bible Discovery

### *The Impact of Chaos in Our World*

The creation story clearly demonstrates God's power over chaos. Merely by the power of his words, God set boundaries for chaos and brought shalom to the universe. But no sooner had God's beautiful creation been put in order than chaos, in the form of the crafty serpent, reared its ugly head (Genesis 3:1). With the simple question, "Did God really say ...?" the people God had created were invited to choose the story of chaos over God's story of shalom.

1. God created Adam and assigned a role for him to fulfill in the Garden of Eden. What was Adam's task, and in what ways could it be considered to be a type of partnership with God? (See Genesis 2:8 – 9, 15 – 17.)

What happened to that partnership when Adam and Eve accepted the serpent's invitation to participate in his story rather than God's story? (See Genesis 3:1 – 10.)

What resulted from Adam and Eve's disobedience and their rejection of God's partnership, and in what ways are these consequences a return of chaos? (See Genesis 3:14 – 19.)

2.  Chaos starts with an individual choice to choose sin over partnership with God and his story, but it doesn't end there. When humans are sinful individually, they begin to create relationships, systems, and structures that are based on evil and devoted to evil. This results in corporate, as well as individual, chaos. Notice the progression of sin and chaos in the ordered, harmonious world God had created.

    a.  What form did chaos take in Adam and Eve's family? (See Genesis 4:1 – 8.)

    b.  How extensive had chaos become by the time of Noah? (See Genesis 6:5 – 7.)

c.  What were people committed to doing in order to preserve and build up their own culture of chaos at the time of the tower of Babel? (See Genesis 11:1 – 9.)

d.  When chaos becomes so big that it becomes an institution or "kingdom," what can we expect to see happen to people who are on the "outside" of the culture? (See Exodus 1:8 – 14.)

## Reflection

Chaos is something God never desired for his creation. He always intended his creation to exist in perfect harmony and order, and he has a plan to restore that shalom to individuals and to creation itself. When those who suffer under the brutal evil of "kingdoms of chaos" cry out, God notices — just as he did when "the Israelites groaned in their slavery and cried out, and their cry for help because of their slavery went up to God. God heard their groaning . . . and was concerned about them" (Exodus 2:23 – 25).

What are some of the "kingdoms of chaos" in your world that advance injustice and cause suffering? (Think of political entities, social structures or movements, cultural institutions, financial structures, etc.)

What is the cry of the people who suffer under each of these kingdoms, and who hears them?

What is involved in bringing some of God's shalom into the lives of those who are oppressed by chaos?

Ultimately, the question each of us must ask is, "Where do I stand in this conflict between kingdoms — the kingdom of chaos and the kingdom of God?" What is your honest answer?

Are these kingdoms always in conflict? Is it possible to participate in both kingdoms? Why or why not?

What does it mean for me to "join in" God's story — to be part of the message of his kingdom and to bring some shalom to a creation oppressed by chaos?

## Day Three | Knowing the One Who Keeps the Order

### The Very Words of God

*I will give them a heart to know me, that I am the LORD. They will be my people, and I will be their God, for they will return to me with all their heart.*

*Jeremiah 24:7*

## Bible Discovery

### *Discovering the God of Shalom in the Land of the Pharaohs*

In Egypt, Pharaoh, in cooperation with the gods, kept order. A person couldn't live in Egypt and not know the story of Pharaoh, ma'at, and chaos. So how was the God of the Hebrews going to show them his story? How would they come to know that he, not Pharaoh or the gods of Egypt, was the all-powerful God who kept the universe in order? How was he going to show how much he cared for them and how he longed for them to become eager participants in his plan to restore shalom to all things? Perhaps that was part of God's purpose for the exodus.

1.　God gave Moses a specific message to give to the Hebrews while they were enslaved in Egypt. What was that message? (See Exodus 6:6 – 8.)

　　What did this message say about who had the power to keep order in their world?

　　What did God intend for his people to discover about him?

2.　What was at least part of the purpose for the plagues by which God afflicted Egypt? (See Exodus 10:1 – 2.)

How effective do you think this strategy was in demonstrating to the Hebrews who God was? Why?

For a moment, imagine yourself being in Egypt at this time. How do you think these events would have influenced the importance of Pharaoh's story in your mind? The importance of God's story?

## PROFILE OF A CULTURE
### Pharaoh, Keeper of the Order

In the Egyptian story, the world existed as a "bubble" in the cosmic ocean. Waters surrounded the earth above the sky and below the earth. The sun god Ra sailed across the surface of the ocean above during the day and beneath the earth during the night. Only the gods had the power to keep the "ocean" of the heavens from collapsing and destroying life on earth.

So the Egyptians were very aware of the tension between life on earth and the chaos of the cosmos. If harmony was not maintained, life on earth would end. Harmony was so important that the Egyptians deified it as the goddess Ma'at. The focus of religious ritual in Egypt was to ensure that ma'at, or harmony, would prevail so that life would be pleasant and free from the destruction of chaos. Pharaoh, who was viewed as god incarnate, was responsible to maintain ma'at through his divine powers and by performing the necessary religious rituals.

Although Pharaoh was personally responsible for the daily temple rituals, priests generally performed them on his behalf. There was no way for one person to perform the ritual twice a day in thousands of temples. In general, the ritual performed on Pharaoh's behalf went like this:

**A PHARAOH'S CARTOUCHE. PHARAOH'S NAME, AND ONLY PHARAOH'S NAME, WAS ALWAYS WRITTEN WITHIN THE "BUBBLE" THAT REPRESENTED THE ORDER OF LIFE ON EARTH WITHIN THE CHAOS OF THE COSMIC OCEAN.**

- Pharaoh (or the priest) would purify himself in the sacred lake.
- He would enter the temple and break the seal on the door of the sanctuary where the image of the god was kept.
- He would undress the image of the god and prostrate himself in front of it while singing hymns of praise and asking the presence of the deity to enter the statue.
- He would circle the shrine with incense and make a formal presentation of ma'at or cosmic order.
- He would wash the statue, anoint it with oil, line its eyes with kohl, and redress it.
- He would offer a meal of meat, vegetable, fruit, wine, milk, and beer to the image of the god.
- He would leave and reseal the door of the sanctuary.

It is safe to say that Pharaoh's job of maintaining ma'at by placating the gods was the most important job in Egypt. After all, if he didn't do his job, the whole

*continued on next page . . .*

**THIS ARTIST'S RENDERING PORTRAYS THE PHARAOH OF EGYPT IN THE DAILY TEMPLE RITUAL OF THE GODS. DRESSED AS A PRIEST, THE PHARAOH (SEE ARROW) BRINGS APPROPRIATE OFFERINGS TO THE STATUE OF AMUN RE. AFTER HAVING CLEANED AND ANOINTED THE STATUE, PHARAOH PRESENTS GIFTS OF GRAIN, MEAT, AND FRUIT TO PLACATE THE GOD, WHO THEN KEEPS THE UNIVERSE FUNCTIONING IN A BENEFICIAL WAY.**

universe would collapse! So it shouldn't surprise us that so many wall carvings depict Pharaoh presenting ma'at to one or more of the gods—it was his job. The Egyptians, and perhaps many of the Hebrews as well, believed that Pharaoh maintained the order of the universe and the harmony of daily life by his direct action. Imagine what they thought when God himself challenged the authority (the order) of the gods of Egypt!

3. What motivated God's awesome display of power in redeeming his people from slavery in Egypt, and how would his actions have challenged Egypt's story? (See Deuteronomy 7:7 – 8.)

4. What did God want from his people in response to his great acts, and how would this response make his people part of his story? (See Deuteronomy 7:9 – 11.)

---

**DID YOU KNOW?**

**The Meaning of Yada**

*Yada*, a key Hebrew word in the book of Exodus, is used frequently to express God's desire to be known by his people. However, the word means much more to the Hebrew mind than it means to us. *Yada* isn't limited to knowing something from a rational, intellectual basis; it also encompasses knowing from an intimate perspective that is experiential, relational, and emotional. When it is applied to one's relationship with God, *yada* implies a close, personal experience with God that results in an experiential and relational understanding of his nature.

The first use of *yada* occurs in Genesis 4:1, 25, where the text says Adam *knew* Eve and she gave birth (newer translations may say "lay" or "had relations"), which conveys the deep, close, personal meaning of the word. In some instances, the word translated as "chosen" or "known" (Genesis 18:19; Amos 3:2) is also *yada,* implying God's deep, personal knowledge of those he has chosen. The prophets used *yada* to express how coming disaster would once again cause God's people to know him (Ezekiel 12:12 – 20; 15:6 – 8). Jesus likely used the word when describing his relationship with the Father and the relationship his followers can have with the Father through him (Matthew 11:27).

---

## Reflection

God desires for all people to know him — not just to know about him, but to *yada* him and join in his story. The text provides a beautiful picture of what it means to know God and delight in him when

Jethro, the priest of Midian and father-in-law of Moses, reunites with Moses in the desert:

> *So Moses went out to meet his father-in-law and bowed down and kissed him. They greeted each other and then went into the tent. Moses told his father-in-law about everything the L*ORD *had done to Pharaoh and the Egyptians for Israel's sake and about all the hardships they had met along the way and how the L*ORD *had saved them.*
>
> *Jethro was delighted to hear about all the good things the L*ORD *had done for Israel in rescuing them from the hand of the Egyptians. He said, "Praise be to the L*ORD*, who rescued you from the hand of the Egyptians and of Pharaoh, and who rescued the people from the hand of the Egyptians. Now I know that the L*ORD *is greater than all other gods, for he did this to those who had treated Israel arrogantly." Then Jethro, Moses' father-in-law, brought a burnt offering and other sacrifices to God, and Aaron came with all the elders of Israel to eat bread with Moses' father-in-law in the presence of God.*

*Exodus 18:7 – 12*

In what ways does this picture help you to better understand what God intended to accomplish by displaying his mighty power through the exodus experience?

How does the exodus story help you to comprehend what it means to *know* God?

How does Jethro's response to all that God had done help you to see God's story — his master plan for redeeming creation — and make you want to be a part of it?

If you have witnessed God's power and experienced delight because of all the good things he has done, and if you in response have worshiped with his people in his presence, how has it affected you?

What will you do to:

Become more aware of God's power at work in your world?

Respond in such a way that you know (*yada*) him?

Participate in his story by sharing what you have experienced with others?

## Memorize

*Jethro was delighted to hear about all the good things the Lord had done for Israel in rescuing them from the hand of the Egyptians. He said, "Praise be to the Lord, who rescued you from the hand of the Egyptians and of Pharaoh, and who rescued the people from the hand of the Egyptians. Now I know that the Lord is greater than all other gods, for he did this to those who had treated Israel arrogantly." Then Jethro, Moses' father-in-law, brought a burnt offering and other sacrifices to God, and Aaron came with all the elders of Israel to eat bread with Moses' father-in-law in the presence of God.*

*Exodus 18:9–12*

## PROFILE OF A CULTURE
### The Temples Tell the Story

Egyptian temples, which may be thousands of square meters in area and reach heights well over one hundred feet, are among the most spectacular religious buildings in the world. But they are much more than marvelous examples of ancient architecture and locations for religious worship: they are the sacred texts of the Egyptian story. Every aspect of these structures means something. The overall design, architectural details, and carvings all tell the Egyptian story just as surely as the text of the Bible tells God's story.

An Egyptian temple portrays the peace and harmony of heaven on earth. The wall surrounding a temple represents the barrier between order and chaos: order inside, chaos outside. Thus the mud brick wall surrounding the Hathor temple at Deir Al Medina is built in a wave pattern to represent the watery chaos out of which the gods brought the order of creation.

**THE WAVE PATTERN IN THIS TEMPLE WALL IS
INTENTIONAL, REPRESENTING THE WATERY
CHAOS FROM WHICH THE WORLD WAS CREATED.**

A temple gate, or pylon, was a massive structure that could be nearly 150 feet tall. A notched space in the pylon directly above the gate represented the horizon through which the sun would rise and set, indicating the connection between what happened inside the temple and the rising and setting of the sun. The pylon also represented the barrier between chaos and order. Carvings on pylon walls usually portrayed the Pharaoh defeating his enemies to show how he had defeated chaos and maintained order so that the gods

**THE PYLON AT MEDINET HABU SHOWING RAMSES DEFEATING HIS ENEMIES AND KEEPING ORDER IN EGYPT. NOTICE THE NICHES FOR THE BANNER POLES.**

would bless Egypt. Niches cut into the outer walls of the pylon held poles from which flew great banners that indicated the presence of the gods. Some poles were more than two hundred feet tall! Just imagine what an impressive sight an Egyptian temple would be. It would certainly encourage people to keep their eyes on the gods!

Outside the pylon, a ceremonial road would lead from the Nile to the temple. In Karnak, the road was lined with statues of the ram-headed god with Pharaoh tucked under his chin, which attested to Pharaoh's unique relationship with the gods. Great processions would carry the statue of Amun Re

**THE CEREMONIAL ROAD LEADING TO THE TEMPLE OF AMUN RE**

*continued on next page . . .*

(the god of the sun) on a bark (a boat) from the Nile into the temple. This journey represented the journey the sun makes across the sky, which was thought to be part of the cosmic ocean. A sacred lake located outside the temple provided a reservoir of water for purification and other rituals, and also represented the cosmic ocean. Are you beginning to see how everything about a temple told part of the Egyptian story?

Inside the pylon were three courts, each progressively smaller with more restricted access. The public could enter the large, outer court. It usually contained huge statues of the gods and, near the entrance to the inner court, colossi (standing statues) of the Pharaoh whose service in the temple was deemed responsible for perpetuating ma'at, or order in the universe. This was as close as ordinary people could be to the gods of Egypt.

From the outer court, the public could see the massive columns of the hypostyle hall where only the priests could enter. The temple of Amun Re has 134 columns, some of them seventy feet tall. This inner court was highly symbolic. It was filled with a forest of columns—often shaped like the lotus, palm, or reeds that grew in the swamps of the Nile—supporting the roof. It represented several things: the "bubble" of life within the cosmic ocean that was supported by the gods who kept the cosmic order in place, the primeval swamp from which the gods created life, and the afterlife that was believed to be a sea of reeds. So the hypostyle hall was an important statement of ma'at, the assurance that all was well in the world.

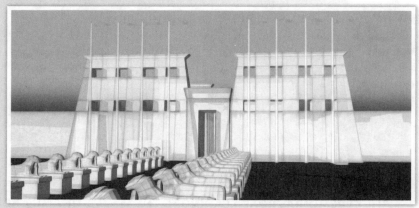

**DIAGRAM OF THE TEMPLE OF AMUN RE IN KARNAK**

At the end of the sacred road, often slightly elevated above the level of the other courts, was the inner chamber or sanctuary, the most holy place in the temple. The sanctuary was a small, dark room without windows where the image of the god was placed. This was where the Egyptians believed the presence of the god resided. It too told part of Egypt's story and represented the mound in the cosmic ocean on which the god Atum stood to draw order out of chaos.

**UPPER RIGHT: JUST IMAGINE THE POWERFUL STATEMENT THE HYPOSTYLE HALL IN THE TEMPLE OF AMUN RE — WITH ITS BRILLIANTLY PAINTED CARVINGS ON COLUMNS AND CEILING — MADE ABOUT THE HARMONY AND ORDER ACHIEVED BY PHARAOH AND THE GODS.**

**ABOVE: A GLIMPSE OF THE HYPOSTYLE HALL CAN BE SEEN FROM THE OUTER COURT OF THE TEMPLE OF AMUN RE.**

# Day Four | The Story Shapes the Culture

## The Very Words of God

> *But they rebelled against me and would not listen to me; they did not*
> *get rid of the vile images they had set their eyes on, nor did they forsake*
> *the idols of Egypt.... Therefore I led them out of Egypt and brought*
> *them into the desert. I gave them my decrees and made known to them*
> *my laws, for the man who obeys them will live by them. Also I gave*
> *them my Sabbaths as a sign between us, so they would know that I the*
> *LORD made them holy.*

*Ezekiel 20:8, 10 – 12*

## Bible Discovery

### *Two Stories, Two Worldviews*

Although there are significant similarities between God's story
about the origin and nature of the universe and his plan to restore
shalom and Egypt's story about the origin and nature of chaos and
order in the universe, there are even more significant differences.
Each story expresses a different, and in many ways oppositional,
worldview, which has significant implications for the society that
believes the story. Worldview matters because it shapes a society. It
defines morality, determines values, and describes proper behavior.
So confrontation is predictable between the people who believe
opposing stories and assume the worldview of their respective story.

1.  The Hebrews knew all too well what it was like to live in a
    culture shaped by Egypt's story. In what ways did the Egyp-
    tian worldview affect the Hebrews, and what indicates that
    God did not share the Egyptian view? (See Exodus 1:8 – 22;
    2:23 – 25; 3:7 - 9.)

2. As you read the following commands God gave to the Hebrews, notice what each says about the worldview of God's story and how it differs from the worldview of Egypt's story. What would a culture shaped by each story be like?

   Exodus 23:1 – 9

   Leviticus 19:32 – 36

   Deuteronomy 5:12 – 15

   Deuteronomy 10:17 – 19

   Deuteronomy 24:17 – 22

3. How essential do you think the exodus from Egypt was to God's plan to restore shalom to his creation? Why?

## WORLDVIEWS IN CONTRAST

| If God's creation story is true, then: | If Egypt's creation story is true, then: |
| --- | --- |
| God exists apart from nature. He created it and sustains it. Nature is respected because God gave it to humans to care for. | Nature itself is god. When nature is worshiped, chaos results because people live for creation and self rather than for God. |
| God commands that the strong care for and protect the weak, as he does. The purpose of strength is to use it to benefit others for God's glory. | The survival of the fittest is nature's great commandment. The strong dominate and consume the weak. The weak suffer under the oppression of the strong. |
| Freedom is available to all of humanity. Those who believe his story work for the freedom of the oppressed. | Freedom is available only to those strong enough to demand it and keep it. |
| God is the source of morality, and society reflects the morality of the Creator, not the creature. | The human mind is the source of morality, and morality becomes whatever Pharaoh (the deified human) decides. |
| All human beings are respected and affirmed because they are made in the image of the Creator. Human accomplishment for the purpose of glorifying God is encouraged, but never worshiped. | The human is deified, and the accomplishments of the human mind and body become the object of admiration and worship. Those who don't meet the standard pay the price. |
| Life is God's gift. The focus of life is to live obediently before God who then gives eternal life to those who believe and live out his story. | What happens in the afterlife is determined by what a person does in this life, so there is an obsession with death and how one prepares for it. |

## Reflection

Worldview makes all the difference in a culture, doesn't it? Perhaps one reason Genesis precedes the book of Exodus in the Torah is because God wanted to make sure his people knew his story. God's story is, in a sense, a critique of Egypt's story and worldview. So it would seem that God wanted to establish his worldview in the minds, hearts, and lives of the Hebrews right from the start of his efforts to restore shalom.

What are the stories that shape the culture and society in which you live?

Which story do you think is most influential, and why?

In what ways does that story shape you, and what reveals its influence?

In what ways does believing the wrong story affect our culture and impact the lives of individual people? (Write down examples of oppression, morality, obsessions, lack of concern, idolatry, etc.)

Which examples of harmony according to society's story do you think are actually chaos according to God's story?

God's story has a message for people who seek to know and obey him today, and part of it is conveyed in Luke 12:22–34:

> *Then Jesus said to his disciples: "Therefore I tell you, do not worry about your life, what you will eat; or about your body, what you will wear. Life is more than food, and the body more than clothes.... The*

*pagan world runs after all such things, and your Father knows that you
need them. But seek his kingdom, and these things will be given to you
as well.*

*"Do not be afraid, little flock, for your Father has been pleased to give
you the kingdom. Sell your possessions and give to the poor. Provide
purses for yourselves that will not wear out, a treasure in heaven that
will not be exhausted, where no thief comes near and no moth destroys.
For where your treasure is, there your heart will be also."*

As you consider these words of Jesus, what connections do you
see to God's story as told through creation, the sojourn in Egypt,
and the exodus experience? Write them down.

What do these connections to God's story have to do with
your role in living out God's story today?

In what practical ways could you, personally and as part of a
faith community, express and live out a worldview that is consis-
tent with God's story?

## Day Five | Take In the Story, Then Live It Out!

### The Very Words of God

*Do not let this Book of the Law depart from your mouth; meditate on it
day and night, so that you may be careful to do everything written in
it. Then you will be prosperous and successful.*

*Joshua 1:8*

## Bible Discovery

### *Taking On a New Identity*

God's call to the Hebrews was not just to leave Egypt, but to leave behind everything Egypt stood for. Until they were completely convinced of the truth that God alone was the one, true, all-powerful Creator who could bring order and harmony to a world that sin had destroyed, Egypt's story would always retain its hold on the Hebrews' hearts. So God had to completely reshape their identity. They had to reject Egypt's gods, its view of chaos and order, its moral standards, its glorification of human achievement and accompanying devaluation of human life, its focus on death, even its leavened bread! All of this was necessary if they were to buy into God's story and live according to its worldview.

God called Israel to love, serve, and obey him because of his mighty acts in Egypt. As you read the following passages, notice how God's act of bringing the people out of Egypt is foundational to their identity, how it molds their understanding of God, and how it shapes their lifestyle.

Exodus 13:3, 8 – 10, 14 – 16

Exodus 29:42 – 46

Leviticus 11:44 – 45

Leviticus 19:33 – 36


Leviticus 22:31 – 33


Leviticus 25:35 – 43


Deuteronomy 6:10 – 12; 20 – 24


Deuteronomy 13:1 – 5


## Reflection

The story matters. The story we buy into shapes who we are individually, and it shapes who we are as a community and a culture.
God's story is the basis for the very identity of all who follow him.
His story is so important that the text says, "Do not let this Book
of the Law [the story] depart from your mouth; meditate on it day
and night, so that you may be careful to do everything written in it.
Then you will be prosperous and successful" (Joshua 1:8).

God tells all who follow him how to live out his story — meditate on
it and do it. But the Hebrew word translated as "meditate" has a far

more powerful meaning than we might expect. The Hebrew word is *hagah* (Isaiah 31:4), and it means to growl, as in the intense, hungry growling of a lion that is devouring its prey! So to meditate on God's story is not to think passively about it; it is to devour it — to take it in, to gobble it up, and then to live it!

How important is God's story to you?

How deep is your passion to take in God's story like a hungry lion?

How committed are you, with the same intense passion as Joshua, to do everything God's story says — to live it out as if you had been there as it unfolded?

## Memorize

*Do not let this Book of the Law depart from your mouth; meditate on it day and night, so that you may be careful to do everything written in it. Then you will be prosperous and successful.*

*Joshua 1:8*

# ISRAEL IN BONDAGE: GOD HEARD THEIR CRY

A visit to Egypt is a stunning experience. The sheer number and magnitude of Egypt's ancient ruins takes one's breath away, and it is difficult to even imagine how long ago the Egyptian civilization thrived. When Abraham visited Egypt, he saw temples that were already ancient! When Moses was born, some of the pyramids were more than a thousand years old!

The landscape of Egypt, dominated by the Nile River, provides striking contrasts of lush, fertile farmland and vast, barren desert. Over centuries, the silt left behind from the annual flooding of the Nile River created amazingly fertile land in Lower Egypt. Even today, decades after the annual flooding of the Nile has been controlled by the Aswan Dam, the land is remarkably fertile.

When God led Jacob and his family to Egypt to be reunited with Joseph and to find relief from famine in Canaan, he led them to an amazing place. Due to the respect and honor Joseph had earned through his service to Pharaoh, his family was invited to settle in Goshen, a prime portion of the Nile Delta. For centuries, God provided abundantly for his people in the most fertile farmland in all of Egypt. Then life in Egypt changed for the Hebrews; they became slaves of a brutal tyrant. Once again, God delivered them, but this time he led them out of Egypt and back to Canaan, the Promised Land.

This raises an intriguing question. Why did God choose Canaan — modern-day Israel — to be the homeland for his people? Israel has fertile places and is beautiful in a variety of ways, but from the point of view of farming and shepherding, it doesn't begin to compare to Egypt. It is not as large, as fertile, and doesn't have the water source that Egypt has. So why couldn't the Hebrews have remained in Egypt? Wouldn't it have been just as easy for God to remove the Egyptians from Egypt and leave the Hebrews there?

No one knows the mind of God (Deuteronomy 29:29; 1 Corinthians 2:11), and he does not specifically answer this question. As we walk in the sandals of the ancient Hebrews and better understand the Bible text in its original context, however, we will gain insight into the Egyptian story and perhaps find some answers.

It was, of course, no accident that God took Jacob's family out of Canaan and into Egypt. During the time period we explore, God was unfolding a purposeful plan, a partnership that required dynamic relationship with a people who would be totally devoted to him. This relationship required interaction with him as God and Lord — total trust in him and his ways. For that plan to be realized, it appears that at least some of the lessons God desired to teach his people could be taught more effectively in a place away from Egypt — first the desert, then the Promised Land.

So what did God do to move the Hebrews out of Egypt, a beautiful and fertile land in which they had lived comfortably and contentedly for hundreds of years? How did God motivate them to leave the security they treasured and the false gods they had come to worship? It wasn't going to be easy. After all, our natural human desire is to choose that which is comfortable over that which is difficult.

God used a cruel Pharaoh who treated the Hebrews brutally. Unable to bear their suffering any longer, they finally "cried out" in anguish, and God heard their cry. In response, he initiated his plan to deliver them not only from slavery to Pharaoh but from their bondage to Egypt's story. As they journeyed to the Promised Land, they would rediscover the story of their God, the God who heard their cry. They would once again become the people of his story, his partners in restoring shalom.

# Opening Thoughts (3 minutes)

*The Very Words of God*

> *The Israelites groaned in their slavery and cried out.*

*Exodus 2:23*

## Think About It

Given the opportunity to live where life is comfortable — where food is plentiful and easy to grow, where it is never cold and snowy, where we can live in safety — versus living in a place where there is political unrest, where it can be bitterly cold, or where people must work hard just to have basic food and shelter, most of us would choose to settle down where life is easier.

But is the "good life" really worth the price? What price do we pay for a pleasant life, not just in terms of overindulgence but in terms of our worldview — how we think about ourselves, God, and others?

# DVD Notes (33 minutes)

### The land of the Nile

### Life in the Village of the Truth

**Buying into Egypt's story**

**God hears their cry**

**God chooses a partner**

# DVD Discussion (5 minutes)

1.  On the map of Egypt on the facing page, notice the Nile
    River and the location of Goshen in the Nile Delta. Imagine a
    narrow strip of fertile land hugging the banks of the Nile and
    expanses of desert flanking that fertile valley to the east and
    west.

    In what ways does the land of Egypt look similar to or differ-
    ent from what you expected, and how does the real picture
    affect your understanding of the story of God's people in
    Egypt and the exodus?

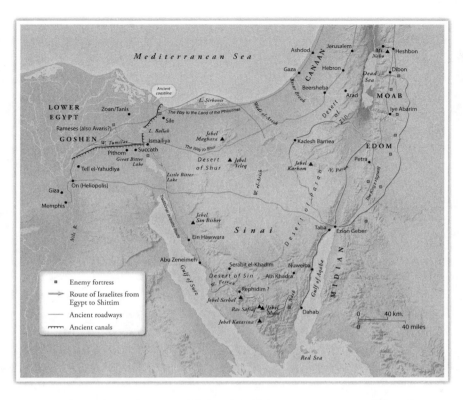

2.  How does the "good life" the Hebrews experienced in Egypt change your understanding of their complaining in the desert? Their longing for the life they had in Egypt? Their attachment to Egypt's gods?

3.  As you consider the many temple carvings depicting Pharaoh's battle scenes and conquests, what do they say to you about what it must have been like to be Pharaoh's enemy?

In what ways do the images of Pharaoh as leader of his people stand in contrast to Moses, the man God chose to be his partner in leading the Hebrews?

**RAMSES WITH HIS STICK SMITING HIS ENEMIES**

## Small Group Bible Discovery and Discussion (13 minutes)

### *The Hebrews Cried Out*

For generations the Hebrews enjoyed a good and pleasant life in Egypt. Their crops flourished. Their herds thrived. Water was plentiful. Their children prospered. Then a new Pharaoh "who did not know about Joseph" (Exodus 1:8) came into power, and the Hebrews' way of life in Egypt changed dramatically. For a long period of time, they were an oppressed people.

1. What motivated the new Pharaoh's attitude toward the Hebrews? (See Exodus 1:9 – 10.)

   What steps did this Pharaoh take to subdue the Hebrews, and what were the results? (See Exodus 1:11 – 22.)

   In this story, who was working behind the scenes in opposition to Pharaoh, and what was the result? (See Exodus 1:12, 17 – 21.)

   What does the failure of Pharaoh's strategy say to you about God's story, and to what extent do you think Pharaoh, the Hebrews, and the midwives realized that another story was being played out?

2. As their suffering became intolerable, what did the enslaved Hebrews do? (See Exodus 2:23 – 25.)

In light of their spiritual heritage with the God of the patriarchs, what was notably absent in their action?

Why do you think they cried out as they did?

---

**DID YOU KNOW?**

The Hebrew word *ze'akah* is translated as "cry out" in English. This strong word implies a desperate outcry made in response to great pain that is usually caused by oppression. God responds with power when he hears such a cry. The Jewish understanding of Exodus 2:23 is that although the Hebrews cried out during their years in bondage to Egypt, they did not specifically cry out *to God* until after the ten plagues.

---

3. How did God respond to the Hebrews when they cried out because of their suffering? (Exodus 3:1 – 10.)

What do these actions reveal about God, his listening ear, and his commitment to his story?

Why do you think God chose a human partner to address the situation when he could have solved it through a mighty display of his power?

## Faith Lesson (5 minutes)

The God of love and justice who is restoring shalom to his creation hates chaos and the sin that causes it. He hears the cries of the helpless and oppressed. Their cries call his attention to chaos, and his great heart of love is moved to respond with power. That is why God heard the cry of the oppressed in Sodom and Gomorrah (Genesis 18:20 – 21), the cry of the Hebrews in Egypt (Exodus 2:23 – 25), and still hears the cry of people today who desperately seek help and hope.

God's story has not changed. He still acts with great power to bring harmony and order to his created world. The question is, will we also hear the cries of those who are suffering? Will we join with God in his story and be his partners in bringing healing, hope, and shalom to people in chaos?

How we answer these questions is important, and the consequences are serious. God described the action of the people of Sodom as being "sin" because they were "arrogant, overfed and unconcerned; they did not help the poor and needy. They were haughty and did detestable things before me. Therefore I did away with them as you have seen" (Ezekiel 16:49 – 50).

1. How do you think God would label your response toward oppressed people in your world such as the poor, the homeless, the hungry, the abused, the prisoner, the single parent, the disabled, the illegal immigrant?

2. What attitudes and actions does God expect those who have been delivered from oppression and the bondage of chaos (including followers of Christ whose sins have been forgiven) to demonstrate toward all people who suffer?

What does this expectation require of you?

## Closing (1 minute)

Read together Jeremiah 22:13, 15 – 16: " 'Woe to him who builds his palace by unrighteousness, his upper rooms by injustice, making his countrymen work for nothing, not paying them for their labor.... Did not your father have food and drink? He did what was right and just, so all went well with him. He defended the cause of the poor and needy, and so all went well. Is that not what it means to know me?' declares the LORD."

Then pray, asking God to give you increasingly sensitive ears to hear the outcry of suffering as he does. Thank God for the privilege of knowing him and pray for an unwavering commitment to obey him and defend the cause of needy, suffering people.

### Memorize

> *"Woe to him who builds his palace by unrighteousness, his upper rooms by injustice, making his countrymen work for nothing, not paying them for their labor.... Did not your father have food and drink? He did what was right and just, so all went well with him. He defended the cause of the poor and needy, and so all went well. Is that not what it means to know me?" declares the LORD.*

> *Jeremiah 22:13, 15 – 16*

# Choosing God's Story

*In-Depth Personal Study Sessions*

## Day One | Going Down to Egypt

### The Very Words of God

> *God spoke to Israel in a vision at night and said, "Jacob! Jacob!"*
>
> *"Here I am," he replied.*
>
> *"I am God, the God of your father," he said. "Do not be afraid to go down to Egypt, for I will make you into a great nation there. I will go down to Egypt with you, and I will surely bring you back again."*
>
> Genesis 46:2 – 4

### Bible Discovery

## *Egypt: Part of God's Plan for His People*

God clearly designated the Promised Land as the place for his people to live and be a blessing to others. Yet often in the history of God's people, some have spent time living in Egypt. What could this mean? How could God's purposes for his people be served in the land of the Pharaohs? What did Egypt provide that another location could not? Consider the Hebrews' experiences and see what you learn.

1.   Where did God first tell Abram (later renamed Abraham) to go, and what was his purpose in doing this? (See Genesis 12:1 – 7.)

2. According to Genesis 12:10 – 13:2; 16:1 – 4, what prompted Abram to go to Egypt?

What insights into the Egyptian story and worldview do you glean from the text?

How did the Egyptian ways affect Abram, and how did Abram's presence affect the Egyptians?

To what extent do you think Abram was motivated by God's purpose during his time in Egypt?

3. When Isaac considered going to Egypt to escape a famine as his father Abraham had done, what did God instruct him to do, and how did Isaac respond? (See Genesis 26:1 – 6.)

What was the result of Isaac staying (as God had commanded) in the land that God had given to Abraham? (See Genesis 26:12 – 25.)

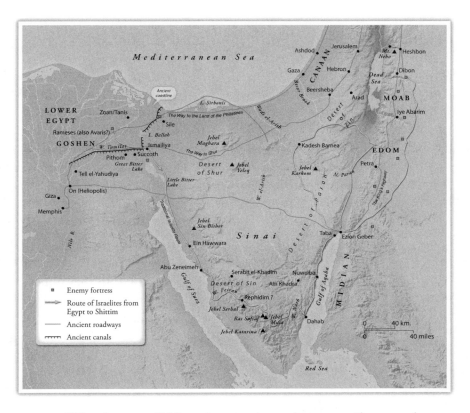

What impact did Isaac's experience have on others, and how would this have fulfilled God's stated purpose for his people? (See Genesis 26:26 – 29.)

4.  Joseph, one of Isaac's grandsons, spent most of his life in Egypt. His experience there had a far-reaching effect on the Hebrews that remains significant for Jews and Christians to this day. You will benefit by taking time to carefully read the account (Genesis 37 – 50) of these experiences. For the moment, consider these highlights:

    a.   How did Joseph end up in Egypt? What was his initial status there? (See Genesis 37:12 – 28, 36.)

    b.   How did Joseph's status change over time, and why? (See Genesis 39:1 – 23; 41:25 – 41.)

    c.   In what ways do you see God's purpose — his people being a blessing in the world, preserving the life of Abraham's descendants, shalom being restored to that which has been destroyed by the chaos of sin — being fulfilled through the seeming catastrophe of Joseph's enslavement in Egypt? (See Genesis 41:56 – 42:2; 45:3 – 15.)

5.   Imagine the shock Jacob (Israel) had when he learned that his son, Joseph, was not only alive but ruling Egypt! Imagine how bewildering it was for Jacob, now an elderly shepherd, to move to a new land with a highly advanced civilization and an ungodly worldview. What was God's purpose in taking Jacob (Israel) to Egypt? (See Genesis 46:1 – 4.)

    From what you have learned about the land of Egypt in comparison to the Promised Land, why do you think this move to Egypt better served God's expressed purpose for his people?

6. How do we know that both Jacob and Joseph never lost sight of God's promise to restore his people to their homeland in Canaan? (See Genesis 47:28 – 31; 48:21 – 22; 49:29 – 33; 50:1 – 6, 12 – 14, 24 – 26.)

## DID YOU KNOW?

When God reaffirmed his promise to provide Abraham with a land and descendants who would become more numerous than the stars (Genesis 15:1 – 7) and cut his covenant with Abraham, God predicted Israel's 400 years of slavery in Egypt! God went on to say that when Abraham's descendants would be released from slavery, they would leave with great possessions and he would punish the nation that abused them (Genesis 15:13 – 14). What insight does this give you into God's story and his plan for his people?

## Reflection

The story of Joseph in Egypt is remarkable in many ways, especially in Joseph's faithfulness to obey God no matter where he was or what the circumstances were. Consider his place in Potiphar's household, for example. God blessed the household of Potiphar because of Joseph (Genesis 39:2 – 6). And when Potiphar's wife wanted to sleep with Joseph and expressed her desire daily, he refused, saying, "How then could I do such a wicked thing and sin against God?" (Genesis 39:9).

What does this reveal to you about Joseph's commitment to God's story?

How well do you think Joseph knew the story, and what do you think it required for him to walk with God in a place like Egypt?

What is your understanding or vision of how God's story is being written in your world today?

What is your commitment to know God and partner with him in reclaiming his world?

In what ways do you think God wants you to be his blessing to people in your world?

How does the location or culture in which God has placed you make it more conducive or more challenging to live out his story?

What do you do to ensure that the "Egypts" of your world — success, consumption, comfort, and pleasure — don't lead you to lose sight of God's story and your partnership with him?

In what specific ways do you communicate to others — your children, grandchildren, faith community, etc. — that it is the vision of being part of God's work that drives us and gives meaning to our lives?

## Memorize

*I am with you and will watch over you wherever you go, and I will bring you back to this land. I will not leave you until I have done what I have promised you.*

**Genesis 28:15**

# PROFILE OF A CULTURE
## The Nile River

Herodotus, Greek historian of the fifth century BC, wrote, "Egypt so to speak is the gift of the Nile." How true! To this day, the Nile River makes life in Egypt possible. Several features of the Nile contributed to its unique impact on the culture of Egypt and the ancient world.

The world's longest river, it flows more than 4,100 miles from its source in the East African Highlands to its delta on the Mediterranean Sea.

The river has two distinct parts: the Upper Nile (Southern) where there is little flat land along its banks and the Lower Nile (Northern) closer to the Mediterranean Sea where flood waters traditionally broadened the river to as much as fifteen miles wide.

**IN THE REGION OF THE UPPER NILE, THE DESERT HILLSIDES COME RIGHT DOWN TO THE WATER'S EDGE.**

As the river approaches the Mediterranean Sea, it splits into several branches creating a delta—a triangle of fertile land comprising nearly 9,000 square miles. This delta includes the 900-square mile region known in Bible times as Goshen.

Prior to the building of dams in the twentieth century, rains deep in the African continent caused annual flooding along the Lower Nile and the Nile Delta from June through October. These floods left behind rich silt, which provided Egyptian farmers with the most fertile, naturally enriched soil anywhere in the world. Thus the Lower Nile is verdant and green all year. The desert begins at exactly the point where the floods (and today, irrigation) end, forming a sudden boundary between arable land and desert.

**FARMS AND FLOCKS THRIVE ON THE ABUNDANT GROWTH MADE POSSIBLE BY THE MOISTURE AND FERTILE SOIL OF THE LOWER NILE.**

In ancient times, the Nile River enabled Egypt to provide food for surrounding civilizations that depended on annual rainfall for successful crops. This is why the Bible mentions people going to Egypt for food during times of famine.

It should be no surprise that this amazing river shaped Egyptian mythology and worldview. The rare failure of floods led to the Egyptian view of a universe in tension between chaos and order. In addition, the characteristics of the Nile and the animals that thrived in it became the source for many of Egypt's gods.

# Day Two | The Best of the Land

## The Very Words of God

> *Pharaoh said to Joseph, "Your father and your brothers have come to you, and the land of Egypt is before you; settle your father and your brothers in the best part of the land. Let them live in Goshen. And if you know of any among them with special ability, put them in charge of my own livestock."*

> *Genesis 47:5 – 6*

## Bible Discovery

### The Hebrews Settle in Goshen

Imagine that you have always lived as a nomadic shepherd. You travel from one watering place in the desert to the next, leading your flocks to tufts of grass scattered amidst the rocks. In the same way that your flocks depend on you for their daily sustenance, you depend on your God to provide the rains that make life possible. Now you have the opportunity to settle in a place where water is so abundant that crops grow even when it doesn't rain, where the ruler looks favorably on you, and where you have been promised the best of the land. What does this mean to you, and how do you use the opportunity?

1.  Where in Egypt did Joseph want his family to settle, and for what reasons? (See Genesis 46:31 – 47:6.)

How appealing would this land have been for shepherds? (See Genesis 13:10.)

After Pharaoh responded favorably to Joseph's request, what did his father, Jacob, do before he left Pharaoh's presence? (See Genesis 47:7 – 10.)

2. What did Joseph's family members receive when they settled in Goshen? (See Genesis 47:11 – 12.)

What did they do with what they received? (See Genesis 47:27; Exodus 1:6 – 7.)

How might this have fit into God's unfolding plan for his people? (See Genesis 45:9 – 11.)

## DATA FILE

### The Land of Goshen

The word *Goshen* is believed to be Semitic in origin and is probably connected with the Hebrew word *gush,* meaning "clod" or "clump," which is a good description of the fertile soil found in the Lower Nile regions. The land of Goshen was:

• Located in the eastern part of the Nile Delta and covered about 900 square miles.
• Not far from the Red (Reed) Sea and the Sinai wilderness.
• Populated by diverse peoples, including immigrants and other non-Egyptians.
• Exceptionally fertile due to the Nile's annual flooding; was known as the "best part of the land" (Genesis 47:5–6).
• The location of Avaris, or Ra'amses, the administrative center for the Pharaohs who are most likely to have been in the dynasties of the exodus.

**WHEN THE HEBREWS LIVED IN EGYPT, THE LAND OF GOSHEN WOULD HAVE LOOKED VERY MUCH LIKE THIS LOWER NILE FARMLAND DOES TODAY.**

## Reflection

It seems that at least part of the reason God brought his people to Egypt was not only to save them from the devastation of five more years of famine (Genesis 45:10 – 11) but to build them up, increase their numbers, and multiply their wealth. Obviously Goshen was a great place for God to accomplish these things among his people. But is it a blessing or a curse to live in a wealthy, prosperous culture where we have more than enough of everything?

Is having everything we want the same as having everything God desires for us? Why or why not?

Deuteronomy 8:10 – 11 describes the great danger of having more than enough: "When you have eaten and are satisfied, praise the LORD your God for the good land he has given you. Be careful that you do not forget the LORD your God, failing to observe his commands, his laws and his decrees."

Why do you think it is so easy to forget God and his blessing?

How can we keep from forgetting God?

Recall a time in your life when God acted with great power and blessed you, and you were very grateful, but then your awareness of his story and your sense of trust, dependence, gratitude, and faithfulness to him faded.

For which blessings from God are you most thankful?

What can you do now to "remember" what God has done, to remember his story and live it?

## THINK ABOUT IT!

Make no mistake about it, the Promised Land was certainly less fertile than the farmlands of Egypt! In the abundance that the land of Goshen provided, it would have been easy for God's people to start believing that their success was due to their own efforts or to Pharaoh and the Egyptian gods. But God wanted his people to learn to walk with him faithfully and to trust him fully for all that they had. So he led them from this fantastic farmland watered by the Nile to the farmland of Israel, watered by rain from heaven — rain that he would faithfully send if Israel continued to walk with him. (See Deuteronomy 11:8 – 21.)

# **Day Three** | Buying into the Wrong Story

### The Very Words of God

> *I swore to them that I would bring them out of Egypt into a land I had searched out for them, a land flowing with milk and honey, the most beautiful of all lands. And I said to them, "Each of you, get rid of the vile images you have set your eyes on, and do not defile yourselves with the idols of Egypt. I am the LORD your God."*

> *Ezekiel 20:6 – 7*

### Bible Discovery

## *Living in Bondage to the "Good Life"*

The Lord brought the Hebrews to Egypt, and there these former nomads enjoyed the best food and prosperity their world offered. Certainly their faith in God blossomed as they experienced his gifts of care and protection, didn't it? Certainly they recognized him as the source of their abundance rather than the Egyptian gods, didn't they? Certainly their part in fulfilling God's plan to deal with the chaos of sin and bring his shalom to all of his creation was greatly advanced, wasn't it? Sadly, as is often the case, that is not how things turned out.

1.  What did God promise Israel (Jacob), and what character-ized the life of the Hebrews in Egypt for generations? (See Genesis 46:3; Exodus 1:6 – 7.)

2.  What insights do you gain from Exodus 35:4 – 29 regarding:

    a.  The skills the Hebrews evidently mastered while in Pha-raoh's service?

b.  The wealth the Hebrews acquired during their time in
    Egypt?

c.  The standard of living the Hebrews enjoyed while living
    in Goshen?

---

**DID YOU KNOW?**

Did the Hebrews work for Pharaoh before they became slaves? No one knows
for sure, but it seems likely because:

- When it came time to build the tabernacle, they were already masters
  of a number of skills that they would have learned only in the service of
  Pharaoh while building his temples, palaces, and tombs.
- It was normal for the farmers of Egypt to work on Pharaoh's projects
  during the months when their fields were flooded. One would expect
  the Hebrews, who lived near the capital city of Avaris, to have done the
  same.
- The text (Exodus 1:10–14) appears to say that what changed for the
  Hebrews was not their work, but the oppression and relentless forced
  labor.

3. What does God expect from those who experience his blessing? (See Deuteronomy 8:10 – 11.)

   Instead of what God desired, what do Joshua 24:14 – 15 and Ezekiel 23:27 reveal about the Hebrews' relationship with God during their time in Egypt?

   For how long after the exodus did Egypt's story still retain its grip on the hearts of God's people? Does this surprise you? Why or why not?

4. After they left Egypt, God's people complained about their hardships and expressed a longing for the life they had left behind. What do their complaints reveal about their life in Egypt and which story — God's story or Egypt's story — had captured their hearts? (See Exodus 16:2 – 3; Numbers 11:4 – 6; 20:4 – 5.)

   Why did they continually want to return to Egypt?

   How great a price for themselves and their children were they willing to risk to regain the benefits of Egypt?

## PROFILE OF A CULTURE

### The Workers' Village at Deir al Medina

During the time of the exodus, workers cutting elaborate tombs of the Pharaohs in the Valley of the Kings lived in a village at Deir al Medina in the desert just west of the fertile Nile Valley. Full-time craftsmen such as carvers and stonecutters provided skilled labor in building the Pharaohs' massive public works projects such as temples, tombs, and palaces. During the annual inundation of the Nile, which took place between June and October, Egyptians who farmed along the Nile (and this would include some Hebrews who lived in Goshen) also worked on Pharaoh's public projects because they could not work their flooded fields.

**ARTIST'S RENDERING OF A TYPICAL HOUSE IN
THE WORKERS' VILLAGE AT DEIR AL MEDINA**

Since the workers' village at Deir al Medina is more than 350 miles south of Goshen, probably few, if any, Hebrews lived and worked there. (Archaeologists have, however, found some Semitic names from the same language background as the Hebrews at Deir al Medina.) It is more likely that the Hebrews worked on similar projects in the vicinity of Avaris, the capital city of the ruling dynasties of the time, which was near Goshen. In any case, the village can provide insights into what daily life was like for the Hebrews of that time and what drew them away from God.

An estimated 250 people lived in about seventy mud-brick houses in the workers' village, called the Village of Truth. The main street ran north and south and may have been covered as protection from the desert's intense summer heat. A typical house had three rooms. The front room may have contained a loom (based on tomb paintings found in nearby workers' tombs), the middle room was used for social gatherings, and the rear room was the sleeping room. An unroofed kitchen was at the rear. Many houses had cellars for food storage as well as stairs, implying that there was a second story or at least a roof that functioned as living space.

**A TYPICAL HOUSE LAYOUT SHOWING A MUD-BRICK PLATFORM (CENTER OF PHOTO). THE HOUSES ARE BUILT WALL-TO-WALL, AND THE MAIN STREET IS THE GAP THAT RUNS FROM LEFT TO RIGHT.**

*continued on next page . . .*

Based on tomb carvings and paintings, it is believed the mud-brick platforms reached by two or three steps that have been found in many houses were likely related to childbirth or child rearing. Still visible in the ruins of this village today, they provide striking reminders of the biblical story of Shiphrah and Puah, the midwives Pharaoh ordered to kill all Hebrew baby boys at birth. Fearing God, the midwives refused, using the excuse that Hebrew women birthed before the midwives arrived.

Stone chips with writing on them, called *ostraca*, reveal much about the lifestyle of the inhabitants who lived here between 1550 and 1050 BC. They were affluent, middle-class workers who typically worked eight-hour days for seven or eight days of the Egyptian ten-day week. They did not work during religious festivals, which is significant because Egypt had more than two thousand gods that were honored in many festivals. In addition to money, workers were paid in wheat and barley, oil, fish, fruit, and firewood. Pharaoh provided water in a cistern just outside the village. Life in this village was very comfortable.

In addition to time off for religious festivals, the people had places of worship such as the temple dedicated to the goddess Hathor located at the north end of the village. Hathor, a fertility goddess, was symbolized by a cow or the

**THE WORKERS' VILLAGE AT DEIR AL MEDINA SHOWING THE TEMPLE TO HATHOR (ON LEFT) AND THE DRAMATIC CONTRAST BETWEEN THE DESERT AND THE RICH FARMLAND OF THE LOWER NILE**

horns of a cow. The highly immoral practices and beliefs of this cult were similar to those of the goddess Asherah, with whom the Hebrews would become acquainted in the Promised Land. In keeping with their skills and beliefs, the workers who built the tombs of the Pharaohs also built elaborate and beautiful tombs for themselves.

## Reflection

Sadly, even though God abundantly provided for the Hebrews while they lived in Goshen, they became enamored with Egypt — its story, its worldview, and its gods. As they experienced worldly "success," they became unfaithful to God and his story, and allowed Egypt's story to became part of them! In a sense, they became slaves *to* Egypt before they became slaves *in* Egypt. They chose bondage to the kingdoms of this world rather than service to God.

Do you think it was possible to live in Egypt, enjoy its comfort, security, and success, and not be seduced by its gods and world-view? Why or why not?

What about the world in which you live? Is it possible to live in and influence your culture without being seduced by it? Why or why not?

What are some of the attractive things that possibly enslaved the Hebrews and can also enslave us?

When does the pursuit of the "good things" a culture offers take on religious qualities?

How do we keep ourselves from becoming so in need of what a culture offers in the way of comfort, success, security, and pleasure that we "buy into" its story — its worldview and value system?

In what sense is it possible to become a slave in a free country?

How do we choose the freedom of being "slaves" to God and his story?

## Memorize

*A man is a slave to whatever has mastered him.*

*2 Peter 2:19*

# Day Four | What Would Motivate the Hebrews to Leave Egypt?

## The Very Words of God

> *So the Egyptians came to dread the Israelites and worked them ruthlessly. They made their lives bitter with hard labor in brick and mortar and with all kinds of work in the fields; in all their hard labor the Egyptians used them ruthlessly.*

*Exodus 1:12 – 14*

## Bible Discovery

### The Hebrews Get Their Wake-up Call

Just as God had promised Abraham, Isaac, and Jacob (Israel), their descendants grew and prospered to become a great nation while they lived in Egypt. Although God had blessed their hard work, their success drew them increasingly toward Egypt's gods. If their later experience with pagan cultures in the Promised Land (or our own experience, for that matter) is any indication, their love for the abundance and prosperity of Egypt lured them away from God and toward the worship of Egypt's gods.

Imagine God's anguish as his people began to forget about him and turn toward Egypt's gods! He had chosen the Hebrews to be obedient partners in his plan to restore shalom to all things. He had called Abraham out of a pagan culture, and now his descendants were so wrapped up in what Egypt offered that they no longer remembered him. They had become slaves to Egypt's prosperity and didn't even recognize it! How would he get their attention? How would he remind them of his story and his plan?

1.  In everything he did, Joseph obeyed God and worked diligently, and God richly blessed his efforts. What amazing accomplishments did God enable Joseph to achieve for the benefit of Egypt and its Pharaohs? (See Genesis 41:46 – 49,

53 – 57; 47:13 – 26.) And what do you think his reputation
was in Pharaoh's eyes?

How might Joseph's reputation before Pharaoh have helped
his descendants?

2.  When a new Pharaoh came into power, what was the status
    of the Hebrews? (See Genesis 47:27; Exodus 1:6 – 7.)

Whether or not they realized it at this time, the Hebrews
were at a crossroads in their relationship with God. What
critical choice were they facing? (See Deuteronomy 8:17 – 19;
Joshua 24:14 – 15.)

Whether or not they realized it at first, the Hebrews also
were at a crossroads in their relationship with Egypt and its
new Pharaoh. What was this Pharaoh's concern, and why?
(See Exodus 1:8 – 10.)

## DID YOU KNOW?

Exodus 1:8 raises questions for modern readers. The Hebrew text indicates that a Pharaoh *arose* "who did not know about Joseph." Because the word *reign* was not used, some scholars conclude that the wording indicates a change in dynasty or ruling family rather than simply a new ruler within a dynasty. This is certainly possible because prior to the exodus, the Hyksos, an Asiatic people, ruled Egypt for about 150 years. When the Egyptians regained power, a change in dynasty would occur.

Given the Egyptians' obsession with recording history, it is also curious that an educated Pharaoh would not have known about Joseph. It is more likely that this Pharaoh did not respect Joseph's accomplishments and his people. This too could be related to the conflict between the Hyksos and the Egyptians. The Hyksos were hated by many Egyptians, and the Hebrews were from the same Semitic race as the Hyksos. So a later Egyptian Pharaoh could easily distrust and be disdainful of the Hebrews.

3. What strategies did the new Pharaoh implement to accomplish his will with the Hebrews? (See Exodus 1:11 – 22.)

What did these strategies actually accomplish, and why?

How was God using Pharaoh's strategies to accomplish his own will with the Hebrews, and what impact do you think it may have had?

What is the difference between Pharaoh's motivation for the Hebrews' suffering and God's?

## REMEMBER THE NAME!

What makes a person important in God's perspective? Apparently not what we might think. When Moses and Aaron first approached Pharaoh about going into the desert to hold a festival for their God (Exodus 5:1 – 2), he answered, in effect, "Who is God? I don't know him, and I will not do what he says!" So it is interesting to note that in the Hebrew text the powerful Pharaoh who ordered the deaths of the infant Hebrew boys is never named, yet the lowly, faithful midwives who refused to comply with his command are (Exodus 1:15)! Might this omission be a response to Pharaoh's claim that he did not know the Hebrews' God? Might this hint at the Pharaoh's insignificance and ultimate lack of power in comparison to the God of the universe and the people who join with him to accomplish his purpose?

NOTE: The Hebrew text can be translated as "Hebrew midwives" or "midwives to the Hebrews." Jewish tradition maintains that these women were either Asiatics or Egyptians, since it is unlikely that Pharaoh commanded the Hebrews to kill their own males. Having only two midwives for the many Hebrews is also unlikely, so Shiphrah and Puah may have been leaders of the midwives.

4. What was God's reason for taking the Hebrews out of Egypt, and how does it fit into his story? (See Exodus 29:45 – 46.)

In Hebrew, the word for "Egypt," *mitzraim*, means "bondage." So reread the passage and consider: What was enslaving about Egypt, and why would it have prevented God from living among them?

**DID YOU KNOW?**

In the exodus story, Egypt is called "the land of slavery" (literally "house of slaves") nine times (Exodus 13:3, 14; 20:2; Deuteronomy 5:6; 6:12; 7:8; 8:14; 13:5, 10). Also note Joshua 24:17, Judges 6:8, Jeremiah 34:13, and Micah 6:4 referring back to the exodus.

## Reflection

It is easy for us to fault the ancient Hebrews for turning away from God in Egypt and losing their distinctiveness as God's people. We can look back and see how they became slaves to their own comfort and credited their "success" to their own efforts and the benevolence of Egypt's gods rather than to God's faithfulness. Sadly, we are not as different from them as we might like to be.

We also are tempted to become slaves to our wants rather than being content with God's faithful provision for our needs. Unless life is difficult for us, we tend to forget, or fail to recognize, our dependence on God. We too lose sight of the great things he has done for us and turn to worship other gods (Deuteronomy 8:10 – 20).

What evidence do you see in your world today that individual people or a culture have forgotten the God of the universe and are in bondage to other "gods"?

How does bondage to the things of this world keep people from experiencing, knowing, and obeying God?

For what reasons did God take away his people's comfort and allow them to experience such terrible pain?

What does this say to you about how important he considers his story, the restoration of shalom, to be?

What kinds of situations compel people to recognize their need for God and fuel their passion to live in obedience to him?

If God treated people who are unfaithful to him today in the same way he treated the ancient Hebrews, what do you think would happen?

Do you think God has or will do this? What would be an example?

How can we know when God is using pain to change us and shape us for better service as his partners in his story?

## PROFILE OF A CULTURE

### The Hyksos

The Hyksos were an Asiatic people of the same Semitic race as the Hebrews. Their name comes from two Egyptian words: *Heka,* meaning "chief," and *Khoswe,* meaning "rulers of foreign lands." Thousands of these people migrated into the Nile Delta between 2200 and 2000 BC, before the time of Joseph. Their presence in Egypt was so significant that when the ruling Egyptians tried to put an end to this influx of foreigners, they were defeated. Thus the Hyksos dynasty of Pharaohs began ( ca. 1720 BC).

The city of Avaris (later, Ra'amses), near Goshen, served as the Hyksos' capital. Archaeological evidence attests to Semitic influence in building design, town layout, pottery style, and burial practices. In addition, bones (but not pig bones!) from animal sacrifices have been found in a temple there, which is unusual for Egyptian religious practice but common in Semitic cultures. Apparently the Hyksos worshiped the Egyptian god Seth (god of foreigners, storms, chaos, and desert), who resembled their own god, Baal.

The Hyksos were powerful. They apparently developed superior weapons such as the battering ram, composite bow, and the horse-drawn chariot that gave their Pharaohs their greatest strength. Egypt generally prospered

*continued on next page . . .*

under the Hyksos who maintained the native Egyptian language, allowed Egyptians to serve in the government, and permitted worship of traditional Egyptian gods. But they were also hated by the Egyptians because of their brutal treatment of their opponents, including the many Egyptians they killed or enslaved. An inscription carved in one of Queen Hatshepsut's temples nearly 100 years after the expulsion of the Hyksos described how they had nearly ruined her country.

Prior to the exodus, Kamose, a native Egyptian, led a revolt against the foreigners (ca. 1540 BC). His son, Ahmose, captured Avaris and chased the Hyksos into Canaan. Reuniting Egypt, he began a new dynasty, one the people of the Bible would come to know well. His dynasty expended great effort to erase all vestiges of Semitic presence in Egypt and developed policies to ensure that Egypt would remain Egyptian.

No matter which date one assigns to the exodus (scholars disagree vehemently), the Hyksos era falls before it. So it is likely that Joseph stood before a Hyksos Pharaoh and with God's help interpreted his dreams. The fact that Pharaoh was likely of the same race and cultural background as Joseph fits the story well. It is also likely that the Pharaoh "who did not know about" Joseph was a native Egyptian who remembered the suffering at the hands of the Hyksos. He would have had reason to dislike and distrust the Hebrews because they shared the same racial background as the Hyksos. His fear that the Hebrews would join Egypt's enemies and defeat Egypt in war probably had a significant basis in reality. Determined to prevent such a threat, Pharaoh attempted to neutralize the Hebrews by enslaving them and purging their male children.

The God of the Bible shapes the affairs of nations in order to bring about his plan of restoration for his creation. By his hand, a simple Hebrew shepherd became the second most powerful person in the ancient world and paved the way for Abraham's descendants to become a great nation. The internal struggles for control of Egypt, which preceded the story of Moses and the Hebrews, were certainly part of God's purpose.

# **Day Five** | God Chose a Partner with a Heart Like His

## The Very Words of God

> *The LORD said, "I have indeed seen the misery of my people in Egypt. I have heard them crying out because of their slave drivers, and I am concerned about their suffering.... So now, go. I am sending you to Pharaoh to bring my people the Israelites out of Egypt."*

*Exodus 3:7, 10*

## Bible Discovery

### *God Chose Moses to Be His Partner*

When God acts to advance his redemptive plan, he often chooses a human instrument — Moses, in the case of the exodus — to be his partner. Through the faithful obedience of this humble and compassionate man, God shaped Israel into a faithful nation that trusted him fully and was prepared to be his partner in demonstrating to the world that he alone is God. But who was this Moses, and what made him a suitable partner for God's next steps in bringing shalom to his creation?

1.  Moses' parents had unusual names for people who were born into slavery. His mother was named Jochebed, which means "praise the Lord." His father was named Amram, which means "exalted nation or people." What do these names reveal about the faith of Moses' grandparents, and how might their obedient walk with God have influenced Moses? (See Exodus 2:1; 4:14; 6:16 – 20.)

2.  The circumstance of Moses' birth and early life were unique
    also. Pharaoh's edict demanded that he be thrown into the
    Nile at birth, but what did his parents notice about him? (See
    Exodus 2:1 – 4; Hebrews 11:23.)

    What steps did Moses' mother take to protect her son?

    It is interesting to note that the word translated "basket" in
    English is "ark" in Hebrew. The only other place the word is
    used in Scripture is when Noah and his family went into the
    ark to be saved from the flood. In what way might this usage
    indicate that God was about to make a move in restoring
    shalom to his creation and that Moses was to be part of the
    plan?

3.  Even though he was raised as the son of Pharaoh's daughter,
    Moses also knew God's story. How deep was his commit-
    ment to knowing God and choosing to be a part of his story?
    (See Hebrews 11:24 – 28.)

    How do you think he learned God's story?

What was he willing to give up to be a part of it?

4.  What character qualities did Moses exhibit that showed he had a heart like the heart of God? (See Exodus 2:11 – 19; 32:30 – 32.)

Who else in the Scriptures exhibited these characteristics? (See Matthew 11:28 – 30; Luke 23:34; John 8:1 – 11.)

NOTE: Whether or not God wanted Moses to "smite" the Egyptian is a difficult issue. My view is that God did not want Moses to lead by "smiting," although God sometimes did that. Far more often, God exercises his mercy and patience.

5.  What do you think made Moses uniquely qualified to partner with God and go to Pharaoh — his Hebrew nationality? nearly forty years of palace life? the finest education? great political connections? forty years leading sheep? (See Acts 7:20 – 23, 29 – 30.)

In contrast, what did God say about Moses' qualifications for the task ahead of him? [Hint: did God mention any?] (See Exodus 3:10 – 14.)

Where did God say Moses was to place his trust and gain confidence? (See Exodus 4:10 – 17.)

## THINK ABOUT IT
### God's Hand at Work

We often focus our attention on the work of the people whom God chooses as his partners in accomplishing his plan rather than on the work God is doing. But God is always working alongside his partners to fulfill his plan. We miss so much of the story when we overlook the ongoing work of God's amazing hand. Consider just a few examples:

The birth stories of a number of people — Isaac, Samuel, Samson, John the Baptizer, Jesus — who partnered with God in his plan to reclaim his world involved powerful acts of God. Moses was no exception. Who but God would arrange for Pharaoh's daughter to defy her father's command and save the very child God would use to punish the Egyptian dynasty, break the power of Egypt, and free the Hebrews?

Think too of the name she gave him: Moses (Hebrew *moshe*), which means "draw or pull out." Unknowingly, as God worked his plan, she gave Moses the name of his destiny — to draw out God's people from Egyptian slavery and the Egyptian worldview they had adopted.

How was Moses exposed to God's story? Where did he get his compassion and the passion and strength to stand against injustice? Although we don't know the answer, God surely was at work teaching him more than the story of Egypt that he would have learned in Pharaoh's palace.

Notice too that although Pharaoh emphasized the killing of baby boys, many of the key people God used to begin the process of the exodus (Exodus 1 – 2) were women — Jochebed, Miriam, the midwives Shiprah and Puah, and Pharaoh's daughter. Pharaoh seriously underestimated the pivotal role women play in partnering with God.

## Reflection

God could have revealed himself powerfully to Pharaoh and the Hebrews without the help of any person, yet he chose Moses to *be* his message as well as to *bring* his message. Think about the messengers God chose throughout the Scriptures and how often he required them to not only bring the message but to be the message. God still has a message to share with the world. The question is, are we willing to be the message as well as to bring the message?

How do you think living God's message made the words Moses spoke that much more effective?

In what ways do you think it was hard for Moses to be God's messenger?

What did it require of him?

What price did he pay for obeying God?

What kind of person do you think God desires to partner with in reclaiming his world today?

What message has he given us, and how has he asked us to *be* the message?

Are you one of God's partners in confronting sin and chaos, in bringing shalom to your world?

If so, what is your specific message, and how do you live it?

Is any part of your life exempt from this partnership? Why?

What does it require of you to be God's partner, and what makes it worth the price?

## Memorize

*We are therefore Christ's ambassadors, as though God were making his appeal through us.*

**2 Corinthians 5:20**

# FINGER OF GOD: THE PLAGUES

Few stories recorded in the Bible are better known than the ten plagues described in the book of Exodus. The Bible portrays these plagues as miraculous acts of God's judgment that occurred in Egypt at a specific time in history and freed the enslaved Hebrews to serve him. The foundational premise of this study is that these plagues occurred as the Bible says they did.

A number of scholars, however, attempt to prove that these plagues were simply natural disasters or that the entire story is a myth. They postulate that Egypt, as the dominant world power during that time in history, simply would not have allowed a large number of slaves to revolt and escape. This perspective is a consequence of rejecting the Bible as God's supernatural revelation into human history. Yet if we consider the points raised by these skeptics, the biblical story becomes even more amazing. Certainly the Egyptian Empire was at the peak of its power at the time of the exodus, regardless of which Pharaoh Moses confronted. And yes, the idea of slaves revolting and escaping Egypt's grasp is far-fetched. It's all quite impossible — unless God actually accomplished what the Bible says he did.

It is truly astounding that the biblical account describes the deliverance of the Hebrews from Egypt without using such words as *revolt* and *escape*. Moses — or God, actually — *brought* Israel out of Egypt, but the text records that the Egyptians *drove* them out of Egypt (Exodus 12:39) just as Pharaoh had "driven" Moses and Aaron out of the palace (Exodus 10:11). The Hebrew slaves didn't have to revolt or escape; Egypt wanted them to be gone!

God acted so powerfully and dramatically through the ten plagues that there could be no mistake about who he was. By demonstrating his power to affect the function of the natural world, God clearly demonstrated that he was the most powerful of all gods and that his good will was essential to their very lives. Both Hebrews and Egyptians discovered that the God of the Hebrews, the Creator of the universe, was greater than Egypt's gods. They experienced God's patience as well as his power. They received opportunities to submit to God's power and authority — ten times! They discovered that God will not be prevented from accomplishing his purpose, and that the Hebrews were to be his partners in fulfilling that purpose.

Why did God choose to use ten different plagues to communicate his message? Were they simply random displays of his power? Or was he using the plagues to teach specific lessons? This study will explore these possibilities, but it will focus on God's intent and purpose for these mighty acts. He was sending a powerful message to anyone who would hear: Israelite, Egyptian, foreigners, and even Pharaoh. Exactly as God predicted, however, many people — including Pharaoh — did not listen. And when you think about it, why should Pharaoh have listened? He was considered to be god-on-earth, the proclaimed incarnation of Amun Re, and he acted exactly in character when he refused to acknowledge that the God of the Hebrews had dominion over all of creation, including the Pharaoh of Egypt.

Like everyone else who witnessed these amazing acts of God, Pharaoh had no excuse. God acted against the gods of Egypt to show his power — to Israel, to Egypt, to Pharaoh — so that they and ultimately all of the world would *know* that he is the one and only God, Creator of the universe. Pharaoh knew. He had seen who God was, but he hardened his heart. The Hebrews, on the other hand, saw who God was and, in grateful worship, left Egypt behind and submitted to God's invitation to join his story and fulfill his purpose.

# Opening Thoughts (3 minutes)

*The Very Words of God*

> *The magicians said to Pharaoh, "This is the finger of God."*

> *Exodus 8:19*

## Think About It

Think of people in your world who have the greatest power. What are the signs of power, authority, and greatness that identify them — dress, occupation, behavior, relationships, lifestyle, accomplishments?

In what ways do powerful people demonstrate their status in relationship to one another, particularly when they are engaged in competition or conflict?

**THE GIANT STATUES OF RAMSES, PICTURED IN THIS ARTIST'S RENDERING OF THE ENTRANCE OF THE RAMESSEUM, MADE A POWERFUL STATEMENT ABOUT THE PHARAOH'S GREATNESS.**

## DVD Notes (36 minutes)

**The Ramesseum: portrait of Pharaoh's greatness**

**The "stick" or "staff," symbol of authority**

**Are you listening?**

**God executes judgment on Egypt's gods**

**Responding to God's mighty acts: the finger of God**

# DVD Discussion (5 minutes)

1.  As you have learned more about Egypt's story as portrayed in the Ramesseum and Medinet Habu, what has impressed you about the role of Pharaoh in that story?

    What insight have you gained into Pharaoh's beliefs about himself?

    What was at stake for Pharaoh when Moses and Aaron walked into his life and expressed the request of the God of the Hebrews?

2.  How important were the "sticks" of Moses and Aaron, Pharaoh, and his magicians to this part of the exodus story?

    What did each "stick" represent?

    What did the specific use of each "stick" mean in relationship to the other "sticks"?

## PROFILE OF A CULTURE
### The Raised Arm of Pharaoh
In this carving, Pharaoh is portrayed destroying his enemies by swinging a mace. Carvings such as these, which are common to many Pharaohs, illustrate Pharaoh's brutal strength in crushing all opposition. In the Egyptian metaphor, to raise one's arm is to display great power.

3.  The Egyptian Empire was great in size as well as in power. Look at the map of Egypt on the facing page and note its great cities and pyramid and temple sites. Consider the number of people who were affected by Egypt's story and imagine what impact the plagues would have on people from one end of the empire to the other. For what purpose did God display his power and authority through the plagues to each of the following?

    Pharaoh?

    The Egyptians?

The gods of Egypt?


The Hebrews?


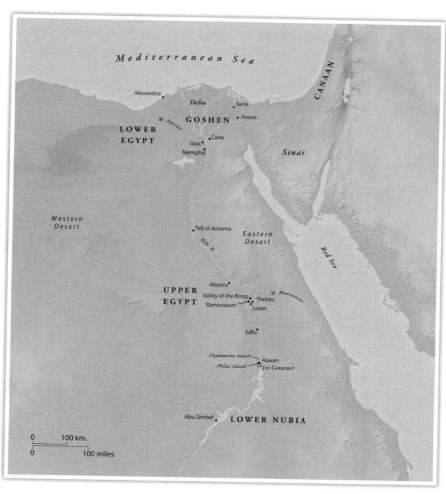

**THE NILE VALLEY**

# Small Group Bible Discovery and Discussion (11 minutes)

## The "Finger of God" Strikes Against Egypt's Gods

Pharaoh represented and wielded absolute power and authority over all the affairs of Egypt and its people. The huge statue of Pharaoh and massive gates in the Ramesseum illustrate his power, as do many carvings showing Pharaoh with an arm raised to crush any and all opposition. Acting on behalf of the Egyptian gods, Pharaoh was responsible to keep the universe functioning harmoniously, and when he exercised his power it affected all aspects of ancient Egyptian life. So imagine how devastating it was to Pharaoh, his magicians and officials, and the entire Egyptian way of life when the humble shepherd, Moses, made his request on behalf of the Hebrews' God, who responded with unprecedented power when Pharaoh dared to refuse.

1. In the visual language of ancient people, Pharaoh ruled his land with a strong and powerful arm. As Pharaoh's slaves, and in a sense his enemy, the Hebrews knew the power of Pharaoh's arm all too well. To clearly express his message to Moses, the Hebrews, and eventually all of Egypt, which cultural metaphors did God use to describe the power and coming judgment (plagues) he would use against Pharaoh and Egypt's gods? (See Exodus 3:19–20; 6:1, 6–8.)

2. How did God say the Egyptians would know that he was the Lord? (See Exodus 7:3–5.)

How might this relate to what God commanded Aaron to do before turning the Nile into blood and starting the plagues of frogs and gnats? (See Exodus 7:19 – 21; 8:5 – 6, 16 – 17.)

How do we know the Egyptians would have understood these actions to be a challenge to the power of Pharaoh and their gods? (See Exodus 7:22; 8:7, 18.)

3.  By what authority did Moses communicate to Pharaoh, and what did Pharaoh's rejection of these messages mean? (See Exodus 5:1 – 2; 6:28 – 29.)

## DID YOU KNOW?

More than four hundred times, prophets of the Hebrew Bible not only acknowledged that they had received a message that was not their own, but that the message came with the full authority of God who was speaking through them. So when a prophet receives a message from God, he speaks the very words of God. When the prophet speaks, it is as if God himself is speaking. (See 1 Kings 21:17 – 19; 2 Kings 7:1; Isaiah 37:6; 38:1; Jeremiah 4:3; Ezekiel 11:5; Amos 3:12; Micah 3:5; Zechariah 1:16; Malachi 1:4.)

4. Who among the Egyptians first understood the awesome power at work in the plagues? (See Exodus 8:18 – 19; 9:19 – 20.)

Which significant metaphor did they use to describe God's power?

What action did at least some Egyptians take when they recognized God's power?

## THINK ABOUT IT

God began the great redemption of his people through whom he would restore all things with a mighty demonstration of his power — the work of the finger of God. The emphasis of this metaphor is that even God's finger displays unimaginable power. The kingdom of God, in which God's shalom reigns over chaos and sin, begins when God acts with power, with his finger. It is interesting to note that Jesus used this same metaphor to describe his powerful saving work in Luke 11:14 – 20. What do you think Jesus' Jewish audience would have thought about when Jesus said he was driving out demons "by the finger of God," and that meant that "the kingdom of God has come to you"?

# PROFILE OF A CULTURE
## Understanding the Metaphors of Power

In the cultures of the ancient Egyptians and Hebrews, people often expressed their worldview and understanding of how the universe worked through visual and sensory images. The Egyptians, for example, told the story of their deities and their Pharaoh through the structure and carvings of their temples. These images were metaphors for what they believed. The spread wings of the vulture (Nekhbet) was the metaphor of Pharaoh's protection, the raised arm and stick the metaphor of Pharaoh's power. The Hebrews used the images of shepherd and father as metaphors to express God's watchful care over them.

We can see one metaphor of Pharaoh's greatness in the huge gates of the Ramesseum. Such gates were built not only to match the scale of the building but to communicate the power of the deity—in this case Ramses the Great as Amun Re—the sun god. Egyptians walking through the gates were reminded of how big the god must be to need such a gate. They also believed that the presence of the statue of the deity removed the heaviness of the heart (sins?) of anyone who passed through the gate. Other architectural features of the temple—huge colossi (statues), extremely high ceilings, gigantic carved footprints—served to emphasize the greatness of Pharaoh and the gods.

**THIS DRAMATIC GATE IS A SIDE ENTRANCE TO THE HYPOSTYLE HALL OF THE RAMESSEUM, THE FUNERARY TEMPLE OF RAMSES THE GREAT. NOTICE THE TWO DOORPOSTS OR PILLARS, AND THE LINTEL, OR GATE HEAD, OVER THE TOP.**

*continued on next page . . .*

It is interesting that the Bible presents God's greatness using similar visual metaphors. Solomon described God as being too large for his temple (1 Kings 8:22 – 27). In Isaiah's vision of God, he observed that merely the end of God's robe "filled the temple" (Isaiah 6:1). David described God — "the King of glory" — as being so majestic and mighty that ancient gate heads and doors would have had to be lifted up in order to prepare for his coming (Psalm 24:7 – 10). Just imagine how great an impression of power that image would have made on someone who had actually seen one of these gates!

So it is not surprising that God revealed his power through the metaphor of devastating plagues. People of that day actually would have expected such an approach. They would have clearly understood the greatness of God's power and his supremacy over all other powers. His greatness was undeniable to all who experienced or heard about the plagues. No wonder they still have an impact on people who read about them.

## Faith Lesson (4 minutes)

The exodus story contains a great irony. The great Pharaoh, who believed he possessed a god's power, refused to recognize the "finger of God" at work in the plagues. In contrast, a simple shepherd, his brother, and then a huge nation of powerless slaves saw God's hand at work and joined God, the supreme power of the universe, as partners in a grand undertaking — to redeem God's broken world from chaos. As a result of that choice, the slaves became far wiser and more powerful than Pharaoh. They would have a hand in returning shalom to God's creation. Today, God still calls each of us to be part of something big — his supernatural, redemptive work on earth.

    1.   What has God done to show you his power and deliver you from the "slavery" of sin?

How do you respond when you see the "finger of God" at work?

What evidence in your life shows your commitment to partner with God in redeeming his broken world?

2. Shalom comes whenever sin and evil, the cause of chaos in God's world, are overcome. What does it look like in your life to be a part of something really big and join in God's redemptive plan to bring shalom into the lives of people around you?

Through which one, small interaction will you seek to bring the shalom of God's kingdom to one person whose life is in chaos?

In what one, small experience will you resist the evil of chaos?

## Closing (1 minute)

Read together Exodus 6:6: "I am the Lord, and I will bring you out from under the yoke of the Egyptians. I will free you from being slaves to them, and I will redeem you with an outstretched arm and with mighty acts of judgment."

Then pray, thanking God for the mighty work he has done to redeem his creation. Thank him for stretching out his arm to redeem you. Praise him for inviting you to participate in the great work he is doing in your world and in your life. Express your heart-felt commitment to join in and be a part of something big — God's ongoing, redemptive work in the world today. Ask for the courage to demonstrate his redemptive power wherever he may lead you.

### Memorize

> *I am the Lord, and I will bring you out from under the yoke of the Egyptians. I will free you from being slaves to them, and I will redeem you with an outstretched arm and with mighty acts of judgment.*

> *Exodus 6:6*

# Choosing God's Story

*In-Depth Personal Study Sessions*

## Day One | The Authority Behind the "Sticks"

### The Very Words of God

> *"Take this staff in your hand so you can perform miraculous signs with it."... Moses took his wife and sons, put them on a donkey and started back to Egypt. And he took the staff of God in his hand.*
>
> *Exodus 4:17, 20*

### Bible Discovery

### *Understanding the Message of Pharaoh's Flail and Crook vs. Moses' Staff*

Anyone who opposed Pharaoh did so at great peril. Many ancient carvings depict Pharaoh holding a flail, crook, or other "stick" and exercising brutal power by beating his enemies or bashing in the skulls of helpless prisoners. Other carvings show piles of human hands, phalli, and tongues being presented to Pharaoh to glorify his divine power over all opposition. The Hebrews experienced the crushing blows of this brute force as they were worked ruthlessly and were forced to throw their newborn boys into the Nile.

In contrast, Moses used his staff in a different way. For forty years, he cared for sheep, speaking to them and leading them to water and safe pasture in the desert. The desert pastures were his training ground where God prepared him to lead the Hebrews out of Egypt. When the time came, God chose to use the ordinary staff that Moses carried as a clear symbol of divine power and calling. Armed with the words of God and the "stick" of God's authority, God sent Moses back to Egypt.

1.  In what ways was Pharaoh's flail and crook, often used in ancient Egyptian carvings to identify him as "Lord" and

"god," a good representation of his authority and style of rule? (See Exodus 1:22; 5:6–21.)

## PROFILE OF A CULTURE

### Crook and Flail: Symbols of Pharaoh's Authority

As symbols of Pharaoh's power, royalty, and deity, the flail and shepherd's crook represented Pharaoh's scepter. In carvings and statues, the flail and crook were usually held, one in each hand, across the chest of Pharaoh or the god Osiris.

*Flail*: A flail was an agricultural tool used to thresh grain. It was made from two or more sticks attached to each other with a chain or rope. After spreading grain on the ground, a farmer would hold one stick of the flail and swing

RAMSES THE GREAT WITH CROOK AND FLAIL. THESE COLOSSI (STATUES) STAND ON BOTH SIDES OF THE ENTRANCE TO THE HYPOSTYLE HALL IN THE RAMESSEUM, THE FUNERARY TEMPLE OF RAMSES THE GREAT. THE NOW-HEADLESS STATUES SHOW PHARAOH'S CROSSED HANDS HOLDING THE SHEPHERD'S CROOK AND FLAIL TO SYMBOLIZE HIS ROYALTY, ABSOLUTE AUTHORITY, AND DIVINE POWER.

the other(s) repeatedly to hit the grain and separate it from the husk. The flail had other uses as well. Soldiers used flails as effective weapons, and the Egyptians used them to hurt enemy captives and slaves.

Because flails were a sign of power, Pharaoh is frequently depicted holding a flail as a symbol of his office. The flail also illustrated his role as the personification of Osiris, the god who was believed to cause the Nile to flood and crops to grow. A flail pictured in Pharaoh's hand typically had three attached sticks.

*Crook*: In hieroglyphics, the crook symbol represented "rule." Scholars believe the use of the shepherd's crook as a symbol of deity, power, and authority dates back to the herding culture of very ancient Egypt. As a shepherd ruled the flock or herd and was obligated to provide for it, so Pharaoh had absolute authority and responsibility to maintain order — ma'at — for the benefit of his people. Eventually reduced to the size of a scepter, the crook often appeared in statuary of the monarchy and many of the gods, particularly Osiris.

2. What action forced Moses to flee from Egypt? (See Exodus 2:11 – 15.)

   How does this incident show Pharaoh's understanding of authority being imitated in the culture of the Egyptians?

   How might this incident indicate Moses' need to be shaped by God in preparation for shepherding the Israelites?

3.  What was Moses doing when he met God by the burning
    bush, and how much of an attitude of authority and power
    did Moses seem to have? (See Exodus 3:1 – 6; 4:1.)

4.  If Moses thought the burning bush was amazing, he must
    have been utterly shocked by what happened next. What job
    was God calling Moses to do, and what authority was he giv-
    ing to Moses? (See Exodus 3:11 – 18; 4:1 – 5; Acts 7:30 – 35.)

    How did God show that he was giving Moses this authority?

    Whose great power accomplished this miracle, and why
    would Moses need to remember this?

5.  In contrast to Pharaoh's style of leading, how was Moses to
    confront Pharaoh and lead Israel out of Egypt? (See Exodus
    3:16 – 20; 4:10 – 17, 29 – 5:1.)

    What did Moses' staff symbolize, and what role was it to play
    in his communication to Pharaoh?

How did the power and role of Moses' staff differ from the power and role of Pharaoh's "stick"?

In what ways does this story of Moses learning how to accomplish God's work influence your thinking about using the power of God's Word rather than the power of brute force in accomplishing God's work today?

## DID YOU KNOW?

### The Message and Authority of Moses' Staff

In contrast to the brute force symbolized by Pharaoh's crook and flail, Moses and Aaron each carried a staff typically used by shepherds. In one sense, that staff was a constant reminder to Moses of how he was to lead. In another sense, it represented God's authority and demonstrated his awesome power over all of creation.

The image of a shepherd leading the flock was very strong in the culture of God's people during biblical times. God's leading of his people is often compared to a shepherd leading a flock. (See Genesis 48:15; Psalm 23:1 – 3; 78:13, 52; 80:1; 95:7; Isaiah 40:11.) Jewish sages taught that a shepherd leads primarily by word, so naturally the words *desert, leader, word, speak,* and *shepherd* come from the same Hebrew root word, *dbr.* Even today, shepherds in the Middle East normally do not drive their sheep ahead of them. Instead, they lead their flocks by speaking to them. It is compelling to watch a shepherd, ahead of a large flock of sheep and goats, talking continually and leading the flock to its destination.

The shepherd provides the image of how God wanted Moses to lead his people, and the staff is the evidence of the shepherd's authority to lead.

*continued on next page . . .*

That's why it was so important for Moses to know that God himself was the power and authority behind his "stick." When God told Moses to throw his staff on the ground and it became a snake (Exodus 4:3), Moses no doubt understood that only God's power could have transformed it—that certainly wasn't something Moses was capable of doing.

It is interesting to note that God sent Moses to Pharaoh to speak to him. It was only when Pharaoh refused to listen (Exodus 5:1 – 2) that Moses' staff became the representation or instrument of the Lord's power in the confrontation between God and Pharaoh and Egypt's gods. Pharaoh certainly understood that the contest between Aaron's staff and the staffs of Pharaoh's magicians (Exodus 7:8 – 12) represented a serious confrontation of power and authority between himself and Egypt's gods on the one hand, and the God of the Hebrews on the other.

## Reflection

Everyone who has accepted God's invitation to challenge chaos and participate in restoring shalom to his creation is, in a sense, a shepherd who leads. That leading involves speaking God's message to family members, friends, neighbors, coworkers, and others so that they will know the one true God and have the opportunity to join in his story. That leading also comes with the responsibility to live out God's style of leadership rather than the kind of leadership Pharaoh demonstrated.

What is your inclination — to lead with power, like Pharaoh, or to lead by speaking the Word of God, like a shepherd?

When have you followed Pharaoh's example of authority and power, as Moses did before he fled Egpyt? What was the result?

What have you done (or what has God done, perhaps without you being aware of it) to learn how to lead like a shepherd?

In Ephesians 6:17, Paul described the Word of God as the "sword of the Spirit," one of the few "weapons" God has given us for accomplishing his work.

In what ways is the Word of God the "staff" of authority and power that unleashes God's redeeming power in our broken world?

To what extent do you know the Word of God well enough to use it for God's purpose?

Why is it so tempting to try to bring about God's work using physical power and human persuasion rather than speaking his Word?

What is your commitment to follow God's leading and learn to live "on every word that comes from the mouth of the LORD" (Deuteronomy 8:2 – 5), so that you can be a shepherd who leads as he leads?

## Memorize

*As the rain and the snow come down from heaven, and do not return to it without watering the earth and making it bud and flourish, so that it yields seed for the sower and bread for the eater, so is my word that goes out from my mouth: It will not return to me empty, but will accomplish what I desire and achieve the purpose for which I sent it.*

*Isaiah 55:10–11*

# Day Two | God's Judgment on the Gods of Egypt

## The Very Words of God

*The Israelites set out from Rameses on the fifteenth day of the first month, the day after the Passover. They marched out boldly in full view of all the Egyptians, who were burying all their firstborn, whom the Lᴏʀᴅ had struck down among them; for the Lᴏʀᴅ had brought judgment on their gods.*

*Numbers 33:3–4*

## Bible Discovery

### God Vanquishes the Gods of Egypt

Why did God use plagues to deliver the Israelites from Egypt, and why did he use the ten plagues he chose? What was the reason behind these catastrophes? In light of what scholars have learned about Egyptian gods, it is likely that the Hebrews and Egyptians would have identified a connection between specific plagues and specific gods. There is little doubt that they recognized the plagues as a "contest" between God's power and the power of Egypt's gods.

1.  God is intent on defeating sin and the chaos it causes in the world and in the lives of people. One way in which he restored harmony to the lives of the Hebrews was to act against the gods of Egypt. What makes the gods of this world, including those of ancient Egypt, a source of evil and chaos, and what is the real power behind them? (See

Deuteronomy 32:16 – 17; Matthew 12:24 – 26; 1 Corinthians 10:19 – 20.)

2.  Since there were hundreds of known Egyptian gods related to the functioning of the universe, any natural disaster would likely have confronted one or more of them. Although several plagues did not directly confront just one of the major gods, all of the plagues indirectly confronted one or more gods. Furthermore, Pharaoh, who was believed to be the incarnation of a god, was responsible for the religious ritual of all the gods, so any and every plague challenged his authority and power.

    As you work through the profile of the plagues and Egyptian gods (see chart on pages 126–127), read the scriptural account of each plague and note the gods that were rendered helpless by it. Then answer the following questions:

    a.  How frightening would the plagues have been to the Egyptians as everything that provided life was destroyed — water, crops, livestock — and the security of their homes and health were corrupted by frogs, lice, flies, boils, grasshoppers, darkness, and death?

    b.  How troubling would it have been for the Egyptians as one after another of Egypt's gods appeared to be powerless before the God of the Hebrews?

    c.  How desperate would they have felt when nothing in their world was left for them to hold onto?

# PROFILE OF A CULTURE

## Ten Plagues and the Egyptian Gods

| The Plague of God's Power | The God(s) Challenged by the Plague |
|---|---|
| #1 Water to Blood<br>*Exodus 7:14–24* | Hapi—spirit of the Nile; caused the annual flood<br><br>Khnum—creator god; god of fertility; guardian of the Nile; deity of water and fertility<br><br>Osiris—God of resurrection and life; Nile considered to be his bloodstream; caused Nile's flood; responsible for fertility of Egypt's farmland |
| #2 Frogs<br>*Exodus 7:25–8:14* | Hecket—frog-headed goddess of childbirth, fertility creation; when frogs appeared each spring, she was believed to bring the new life of spring |
| #3 Gnats (lice)<br>*Exodus 8:16–18* | Geb*—god of earth or dust; worshiped for ability to provide the harvest |
| #4 Flies (swarms)<br>*Exodus 8:20–24* | Nepthys*—the protector of the household; wife of Seth |
| #5 Livestock<br>*Exodus 9:1–7* | Apis—reincarnation of Ptah the creator; bull god of fertility; symbol of procreation and virility<br><br>Hathor—goddess of fertility and sexuality, drunkenness and orgy; the mother goddess; portrayed as woman with cow horns with a sun disc between them, and as a cow |
| #6 Boils<br>*Exodus 9:8–11* | Thoth*—god of wisdom and the moon, medicine and good health, learning and the arts |
| #7 Hail<br>*Exodus 9:13–33* | Seth—god of wind, storm and chaos, evil, darkness, strength, conflict; connected to the desert (chaos); the enemy of Pharaoh (order)<br><br>Isis—goddess of magic, medicine, and agriculture<br><br>Min—god of fertility of the crops and male sexuality |
| #8 Grasshoppers (locusts)<br>*Exodus 10:3–19* | Seth—god of wind, storm and chaos, evil, darkness, strength, conflict; connected to the desert (chaos); the enemy of Pharaoh (order)<br><br>Isis—goddess of magic, medicine, and agriculture<br><br>Min—god of fertility of the crops and male sexuality |

| #9 Darkness<br>*Exodus 10:21–23* | Amun Re—god of the sun; chief of the gods from whom all Pharaohs descended; creator; source of change of seasons |
| | Horus—god of war; provided Pharaoh's power in war; associated with sun and moon; was worshiped with Re as the sun god |
| #10 Deaths of firstborn<br>*Exodus 11:4–8; 12:21–30* | Nekhbet—goddess who protected sovereignty and person of Pharaoh from birth; worshiped in form of vulture with spread wings |
| | Osiris—God of resurrection and life; ruler of the underworld; giver of eternal life |

*NOTE: It is likely that the Egyptians would have thought of these gods in relationship to these plagues, but the connection between these plagues and these gods isn't nearly as strong as the connection between the other plagues and Egypt's gods.

**THE "LESSER" GODS OF EGYPT RARELY HAD THEIR OWN TEMPLES AND USUALLY WERE CONNECTED TO WORSHIP OF OTHER DEITIES. THE EGYPTIANS ARE LIKELY TO HAVE SOUGHT THESE GODS WHEN THE PLAGUES MADE LIFE DIFFICULT. THE GOD OF THE HEBREWS SHOWED HIS DOMINION OVER ALL OF EGYPT'S GODS — LESSER AND GREATER — AS HE DISPLAYED HIS POWER OVER CREATION.**

3.  When the gods of Egypt failed before God's power, as dem-
    onstrated in the plagues, what was God revealing about
    himself? (See Exodus 20:3 – 6; Deuteronomy 11:16 – 17; Psalm
    40:4; Jeremiah 46:25.)

## Reflection

It is easy for us to think of false gods in terms of ancient history, but
false gods are alive and well in our world today. Since long before
the exodus, people have put their hope in many gods other than the
God of the Hebrews. Yet God's desire is for all people to recognize
his supremacy over his creation and to join with him in worship and
dependence on his faithfulness. He still longs for all people to rely
on him and experience the true shalom he offers.

The psalmist expressed the depths of God's desire to be God for his
people in Psalm 146:3 – 9:

> Do not put your trust in princes, in mortal men, who cannot save.
> When their spirit departs, they return to the ground; on that very
> day their plans come to nothing. Blessed is he whose help is the God
> of Jacob, whose hope is in the LORD his God, the Maker of heaven and
> earth, the sea, and everything in them — the LORD, who remains faithful
> forever. He upholds the cause of the oppressed and gives food to the
> hungry. The LORD sets prisoners free, the LORD gives sight to the blind, the
> LORD lifts up those who are bowed down, the LORD loves the righteous.
> The LORD watches over the alien and sustains the fatherless and the
> widow, but he frustrates the ways of the wicked.

Why do you think God would be jealous of false gods who seem
to promise what he offers but do so under false pretenses?

What is it that false gods actually do?

In what ways have you been attracted to the promises of false gods?

What has forced you to reexamine where you have placed your hope?

What happens when you realize you have misplaced your hope?

What have you discovered that false gods offer but that God alone can provide?

In what way(s) do you see God demonstrating his power and supremacy over false gods today?

What is your response to him because of it?

## Memorize

*Who among the gods is like you, O LORD? Who is like you — majestic in holiness, awesome in glory, working wonders?*

*Exodus 15:11*

## PROFILE OF A CULTURE
### The Egyptians' View of Shepherds

We might easily wonder why Moses requested Pharaoh's permission to sacrifice animals in the desert, and not in Egypt. At least part of the reason is because the Egyptians would stone someone who sacrificed a sheep (Exodus 8:25 – 27), and that is one of the animals the Hebrews would have sacrificed (Genesis 15:9). Why would such sacrifices have been an abomination to Egyptians, and why did Egyptians detest shepherds (Genesis 46:34)?

Some scholars suggest it was because shepherds came from the desert, which Egyptians considered to be *chaos*, or because shepherds were considered a lower class. The Bible hints at another reason. The Hebrew word used, *to'evah*, can mean "that which is forbidden for the Egyptians" and "that which is an Egyptian abomination." This suggests that the underlying issue is that gods of Egypt are identified with animals. Although Egyptians apparently did not worship animals, their gods often had animal characteristics — the ram-headed *Khnum* or *Amun-Re*; the jackal-headed *Anubis*; *Hathor* with a cow's horns; and *Apis*, bull god of fertility. Shepherds may have been an abomination in Egypt because they used animals for wool, leather, milk, and meat, hence disrespecting the Egyptian deities identified with those animals.

Just imagine the change that had taken place in the Egyptians and the Hebrews before the tenth plague when, in preparation for Passover, all of the Hebrew households slaughtered a lamb and brushed its blood on the tops and sides of their doorframes! There was no apparent objection to this formerly detestable act on the part of the Egyptians. And the Hebrews apparently had no fear of retribution (or had chosen to listen to their God regardless of the risk). What must the Egyptians and Hebrews have been learning about the power of their respective gods?

**THESE STATUES ALONG THE SACRED WAY OF THE TEMPLE OF AMUN RE IN KARNAK REPRESENT THE SUN GOD AMUN RE, THE KING OF THE GODS IN HIS ROLE AS PROTECTOR OF PHARAOH. ALTHOUGH THE RAM ITSELF WAS NOT CONSIDERED A DEITY, IT SYMBOLIZED THE SUN GOD, WHICH MAY BE WHY EGYPTIANS WOULD STONE SOMEONE WHO SACRIFICED A SHEEP.**

# Day Three | That the Whole World Will Know

## The Very Words of God

> *I will take you as my own people, and I will be your God. Then you will know that I am the LORD your God, who brought you out from under the yoke of the Egyptians.... And the Egyptians will know that I am the LORD when I stretch out my hand against Egypt and bring the Israelites out of it.*

> **Exodus 6:7; 7:5**

## Bible Discovery

### *Knowing the God Behind the Plagues*

In the Bible, *knowing* is not primarily a rational activity, although it certainly involves the intellect. To *know* is to experience a relationship involving deep, emotional connections that are characterized by interaction, loyalty, and commitment. This is why the Hebrew word for "know," *yada,* is used to describe the intimate relations of marriage. In terms of one's relationship with God, *yada* describes a personal experience that results in an intimate understanding of his nature and purpose. Consider what knowing God had to do with the plagues, God's powerful demonstration of judgment on Egypt's gods.

1.  What is God's great desire for people, and how important is it to him? (See Isaiah 45:1 – 6.)

2. The ten plagues expressed God's judgment on the gods of Egypt, but for what other purpose did God display his great power?

   a. See Exodus 7:14 – 17; 8:9 – 10, 20 – 22; 9:13 – 16. Why do you think it was important for Pharaoh, who was believed to be god incarnate, to know that the God of the Hebrews was indeed God of the universe?

   b. See Exodus 7:1 – 5; 9:13 – 16. Why do you think God wanted the Egyptians to know him, and what does this reveal about God's nature?

   c. See Exodus 6:7 – 8. Why was it essential for the Hebrews to know their God?

## PROFILE OF A CULTURE
### Pharaoh's Difficult Decisions

According to the Egyptian story, the universe existed in tension between cosmic opposites: sickness and health, good and bad, barrenness and fertility, light and dark, desert and fertile land. All of life was viewed within the context of the ongoing struggle between chaos and harmony. Ma'at, harmony deified, represented the order that must be maintained in order for the universe to operate smoothly. Pharaoh was responsible for performing religious rituals to ensure that ma'at would prevail and that Egyptian life would be pleasant and not disrupted by the chaos that was always threatening to undo the universe.

Imagine what it was like for Pharaoh to learn about the Hebrew God through the ten plagues! Pharaoh was viewed as Amun Re (the sun god) incarnate. He was the highest power in Egypt and kept harmony intact through his divine powers and religious rituals. So the choice God gave him had huge

**RAMSES PRESENTING MA'AT TO OSIRIS**

consequences. It was not just his personal faith that was at risk. It was his position and his entire understanding of how the universe worked. If he chose wrongly, Pharaoh believed the Nile would not flood, Egypt's soils would lose fertility, and nature itself would be swept into chaos. Egypt and its culture would be destroyed. Imagine the crisis he faced when he stood in opposition to the God of the Hebrews again and again and all of Egypt was destroyed anyway!

3. Moses' opening statement to Pharaoh, recorded in Exodus 5:1 – 2, was a direct challenge from the God of the Hebrews. What was Pharaoh's immediate response to it?

In light of the fact that God didn't end the confrontation immediately, what was he doing for Pharaoh through the plagues?

Why do you think it took ten plagues to free Israel?

When the plagues were over, what do you think Pharaoh knew about God and why he should obey him?

4.  How did Pharaoh respond to God after the last plague (Exodus 12:31 – 32) as compared to earlier challenges (Exodus 8:19)?

5.  What is the difference between the "cry" of the Hebrews in Egypt before the plagues (Exodus 2:23) and their cry after seeing the effects of the plagues (Exodus 14:1 – 10)?

What had they come to know about God during the process?

## THINK ABOUT IT

### What Might God Have Wanted People to Know about Him through the Plagues?

I am the Creator and sustainer of the universe, not Egypt's gods.

I am making a new creation to redeem my world from sin's chaos.

I — and I alone — am the one, true, all-powerful God of the universe.

## Reflection

The heart of God goes out to all people, and he truly desires to be known as Lord. To know God in the Hebrew mind-set is to experience who he is and to respond in grateful worship and faithful obedience to all of his commands. To know God is to become part of his story and to be passionate about living the story and sharing it with others so that they too will come to know God.

In Exodus 34:6 – 7, Moses described God as "the compassionate and gracious God, slow to anger, abounding in love and faithfulness, maintaining love to thousands, and forgiving wickedness, rebellion and sin." In what ways does the story of the ten plagues illustrate to you the essence of God's nature and his desire that every person come to *know* him?

What does it mean to you that God, even after all of the evil that had been done to the Hebrews, had a deep desire for the Egyptians to know (experience) him and be set free from the bondage of their chaos?

What hope and confidence does this give you of God's desire for you to know him?

How can you share this hope and confidence with people in your culture who may think they are too deeply trapped in chaos for God to want a relationship with them?

In preparation for what God had planned, why was it essential for the Hebrews to know him and turn away from the chaos of Egypt's gods?

What is at stake for people today who know about God but are still participating in the chaos of sin?

What do people today miss out on when they know God intellectually, such as through doctrine, but fail to really know and experience him as the one true God?

In the exodus story, God desired that everyone — Pharaoh, Egyptians, Hebrews, foreigners, future generations — know him as the one, true Creator God. How committed are you to:

Know, experience, worship, and obey God?

Know God so well and live for him with such passion that other people come to know him through you?

**Day Four** | The Plagues: Echoes of God's Creation Story?

## The Very Words of God

*If you follow my decrees and are careful to obey my commands, I will send you rain in its season, and the ground will yield its crops and the trees of the field their fruit.... I will look on you with favor and make you fruitful and increase your numbers, and I will keep my covenant with you.*

*Leviticus 26:3 – 4, 9*

## Bible Discovery

### God Begins Creating Something New[1]

It is significant that God gave the story of his creation to Moses to share with the Hebrews early in their exodus journey. They knew their own story — their plight in Egypt, God hearing their cry, the plagues, and their miraculous exit from Egypt — and were beginning to see their role in God's unfolding story. They would have noticed words, phrases, events, and numbers from the creation story that were repeated in or connected to their own story. So what impact would the revelation of God's creation story have on their understanding of what God was doing with them? A careful comparison of Genesis 1 to Exodus 7 – 12 is quite revealing.

1.  When stretching out his staff to initiate the first plague, Aaron holds his staff over the "waters of Egypt" (Exodus 7:19). This same Hebrew word for "waters," *mikveh*, appears in the creation account when God named the "gathered waters" seas (Genesis 1:10). The phrase, "and they will turn to blood," literally means "let them turn to blood," which echoes God's "let there be" commands in Genesis. How do these connections influence your perception of the bigger picture God may have had in mind for the plagues and the exodus?

2. There are a number of parallels and contrasts between what God did in Genesis to create the natural world out of chaos and what God did through the plagues in Egypt to reduce the natural world back to chaos.

| Genesis Creation | The Plagues as "Counter Creation" |
|---|---|
| The waters teemed with life (Gen. 1:20) | What chaos "teemed" from the waters of the Nile? (Ex. 8:3) |
| The land produced living creatures (Gen. 1:24) | What chaos did the land produce? (Ex. 8:16 – 18) |
| Flying creatures are made (Gen. 1:20-22) | What chaos came from the air? (Ex. 8:21) |
| God gave livestock to humans (Gen. 1:25 – 26) | What was taken away from the Egyptians? (Ex. 9:2 – 6) |
| On the third day, God put vegetation on the earth (Gen. 1:11 – 12) | What plagues caused Egypt to look as the earth did before the third day of creation? (Ex. 9:13 – 10:20, especially 10:15) |
| God distinguished light from darkness and created light givers (Gen. 1:3 – 5, 14 – 19) | What chaos reigned in Egypt (but not Goshen) for three days? (Ex. 10:21 – 23) |
| God created human beings (Gen. 1:26 – 27) | In what way did God take back this creation, and what chaos did it bring? (Ex. 11:1 – 8; 12:29 – 30) |

a. In the second, third, and fourth plagues (frogs, gnats or lice, and flies) the creatures of the water, land, and air were totally out of control. How is this a contrast to God's creation? (See Genesis 1:26.)

    b.  By the time the plagues ended, in what ways was Egypt like the chaos that existed before God began creation?

    c.  In what ways do you think this destruction of what had been created may have indicated to the Hebrews that God was creating something new through the exodus?

3.  God could have changed Pharaoh's mind with one plague, forty plagues, or none. So why did he choose ten? We, of course, can't know the mind of God beyond what he has revealed, but there are some intriguing hints that the plagues were establishing him as the sovereign Creator God for both the Egyptians and Hebrews.

    a.  How many times did God speak to create and organize his universe, and what connection do you see to the plagues? (See Genesis 1:3, 6, 9, 11, 14, 20, 24, 26, 28 – 29.)

    b.  The Egyptians had a ten-day week, and there were ten plagues. God established a seven-day week when he created the universe and its inhabitants. How many plagues did the psalmist list, and what might this suggest? (See Psalm 78:44 – 51; 105:29 – 36.)

4.  Genesis 1:28 – 30 pronounces God's blessing on Adam and
    Eve after God's work of creation was accomplished. What
    were his instructions, and what was his promise?

    Toward the end of God's commands for the Israelites
    recorded in the book of Leviticus, what instructions and
    promises does God give? (See Leviticus 26:1 – 13.)

    How does what God expected from Adam and Eve compare
    with what he expected from the Israelites?

    In what sense did God entrust the Israelites with a new cre-
    ation?

## DID YOU REALIZE?

Ancient people were totally dependent on their physical world. They were
quite limited in what they could do to change natural conditions. If drought or
too much rain came, they faced famine. And they had no advance warning
of floods or devastating storms. Furthermore, they did not understand the
function of the physical world as we do, so they attributed everything that
happened to a direct act of a deity. The god who could affect the function of
the natural world was the most powerful of all gods, and his (or her) good will
was essential to their lives. So in the minds of the Egyptians and Hebrews,
the plagues could certainly be viewed as God's declaration that he alone was
the God of creation.

## Reflection

When the Exodus account repeats words and phrases from the creation story, we can go back to that story and consider how God's spectacular actions in Egypt displayed his work in creating a new people, a new creation to continue his plan of redeeming his world from the chaos of sin. Using an "outstretched arm and with mighty acts of judgment" (Exodus 6:6), God did away with the "old," the corruption and chaos his people had known in Egypt. He brought them out to become a "new" creation and bring his shalom to a needy world.

God is still redeeming his creation, and he still invites people to join in his story — to worship him with such awe and faithful obedience that all the world may know that he is the living God! Just as the Hebrews needed to recognize that they were a new creation set free from bondage to Egypt, believers today need to recognize that we are a new creation set free from bondage to sin. Consider the apostle Paul's description of what the mighty power of God has done for us and how he desires us to respond:

> *Therefore, if anyone is in Christ, he is a new creation; the old has gone, the new has come! All this is from God, who reconciled us to himself through Christ and gave us the ministry of reconciliation: that God was reconciling the world to himself in Christ, not counting men's sins against them. And he has committed to us the message of reconciliation. We are therefore Christ's ambassadors, as though God were making his appeal through us. We implore you on Christ's behalf: Be reconciled to God.*
>
> *2 Corinthians 5:17–20*

In what sense is a redeemed person a "new" creation, and what has God done with the "old" creation?

What does God desire from his "new" creation?

How is what Paul calls "reconciliation" like the restoration of shalom?

How is what God desires of his "new" creation like what he desired from Adam and Eve and the Hebrews?

What does it mean to you that God exercised his great power on your behalf to redeem you out of the world of chaos?

How would you describe what he has done for you?

If you have joined in God's story and been made a new creation, how much of your life is devoted to the work of reconciliation — the restoration of shalom — in God's world?

In what places of chaos are you willing to be an ambassador for him?

## Memorize

*Therefore, if anyone is in Christ, he is a new creation; the old has gone, the new has come!*

**2 Corinthians 5:17**

**Day Five** | Did Israel Hear (Act on) God's Message?

## The Very Words of God

*The LORD is my strength and my song; he has become my salvation. He is my God, and I will praise him, my father's God, and I will exalt him.*

**Exodus 15:2**

### Bible Discovery

### *The Hebrews Learn to Listen*

It was one thing for Moses to deliver God's message to Pharaoh and for Pharaoh to close his ears to it. Perhaps Moses expected that. He knew that Pharaoh believed himself to be a god who kept harmony and natural order in the universe, so why would he listen? And hadn't God prepared Moses and Aaron with miraculous signs to convince Pharaoh of the authenticity of their message? But what about the Hebrews? Had they grown so complacent in Goshen and become so much a part of Egypt's story that they too would have difficulty hearing and acting upon God's message?

1.  When the Hebrew elders first learned that God had heard
    their cry and was concerned about them, how did they
    respond? (See Exodus 4:29 – 31.)

    Had they heard God's message? How can you know?

2.  What happened to the Hebrews' willingness to hear God's
    message when Pharaoh's treatment of them became even
    harsher than it had been? (See Exodus 5:17 – 19; 6:6 – 9.)

    What does it mean that God has "pierced" (the Hebrew word
    used means "digging" or "hewing stone") someone's ears?
    (See Psalm 40:6 – 8.)

    What kinds of things plugged the Hebrews' ears so they
    could not hear (act on) God's message given through Moses?

3.  What do we discover in Exodus 14:8 and Numbers 33:3
    about how the Hebrews left Egypt?

    Had they heard God's message? How can you know?

## DID YOU REALIZE?

The animals normally sacrificed to God by the descendants of Abraham included sheep and cows, both of which were sacred to the Egyptians. The ram was the sacred representation of Amun and the cow was the sacred representation of Hathor; sacrificing either animal to another god would be an abomination to the Egyptians and could result in death by stoning (Exodus 8:26 – 27). So it was a huge step of faith for the Hebrews to select a lamb, tie it up for several days, and then kill it in public and spread its blood over their doorposts. As slaves of Egypt, the Hebrews really had to believe that their God would protect them from retribution at the hand of their masters.

4. After being led safely through the Red Sea and delivered from Pharaoh and his army, what did the Israelites sing about? (See Exodus 15:1 – 18.)

   In what ways were they starting to hear the message of their God?

5. Just a few days after the plagues ended and the Hebrews left Egypt and crossed the Red Sea, what happened to challenge their trust in God? (See Exodus 15:22 – 27.)

   What did God want to teach them about the importance of listening to his voice?

What did God desire to do for them, and what promise did
he give to them?

## Reflection

Often we're content to praise God for his mighty acts, talk about
how wonderful they are, then "sit on the sidelines" and wait for
him to work again. But God desires those who hear his message to
express total commitment resulting in action. His desire, expressed
in Exodus 15:26, is for his followers to "listen carefully to the voice
of the LORD your God and do what is right in his eyes ... pay attention to his commands and keep all his decrees."

> When God acts in your life with power (i.e., restored health,
> answered prayer, daily needs met, safety provided, job or schol-
> arship provided, new friends, spouse), what action(s) do you
> think he desires of you?

When have you been most deeply affected by God's power:

> When you have read about his mighty acts in the Bible?

> When you have based your faith on the promise of God's
> Word and then experienced it in your own life as you took
> action?

In what ways has taking action in response to God's voice built up your faith and your relationship with him?

What specific things "plug" your ears so you don't hear the Word of God, and what holds you back from responding with appropriate action?

What will you do to correct any obstacles that hinder your walk with God?

When have you made the effort to listen for God's voice in your life and been passionately determined to do what is right in his eyes?

What has been the result?

## Memorize

*If you listen carefully to the voice of the* LORD *your God and do what is right in his eyes, if you pay attention to his commands and keep all his decrees, I will not bring on you any of the diseases I brought on the Egyptians, for I am the* LORD, *who heals you.*

**Exodus 15:26**

# WATCH WITH ME: ISRAEL LEAVES EGYPT

When the Hebrew slaves cried out in anguish, the God of their ancestors heard their cry and sent Moses to deliver them. But, just as God had said he would, Pharaoh refused to let his nation of slaves go — not even for a few days to make sacrifices to their God. So as a display of judgment against Egypt's gods, the God of the Hebrews brought a series of nine plagues upon the land and people of Egypt. By displaying his supremacy over Egypt's gods, God demonstrated that he alone is the Creator and Lord of the universe.

At least from the biblical record, the Hebrews seemed to have remained strangely silent during these miraculous plagues. It is as if they were merely observers of this cosmic contest. From a certain perspective, their apparent lack of interest or involvement makes sense. They were, after all, slaves, Pharaoh's possessions. Like animals, they did not think or act for themselves. They did what they were told to do, and as long as they fulfilled the requirements, they were cared for.

God had big plans for the Hebrews, however. During the plagues, they experienced God's loving care and, unlike the Egyptians, were spared the destruction of their crops and livestock. And through his prophet, Moses, God had promised to deliver them from the Egyptians' "yoke," to set them free, to redeem and protect them, and to be their God and take them to be his people (Exodus 6:6–7). In order for this to happen, the Hebrews needed to be more than observers; they needed to participate in the story God was unfolding. It was time for them to start becoming a new creation, a new culture, and a new people shaped and molded by their God to make his name known throughout the world. It was time for them to bring shalom — God's order, harmony, and purpose — into his creation and participate in the life of his kingdom.

So, as the tenth and final plague neared, God gave the Hebrews an active role that required them to take steps of faith. God often would ask them to take similar steps in the future. It was a new beginning, and God was making them a new creation. They were on their way out of Egypt, and God was beginning to get Egypt out of them.

The Hebrews were to make a total break from the past. God established a new calendar for them. He instituted Passover laws and commanded the Hebrews to relive the Passover ritual every year. He wanted future generations to remember that first Passover in Egypt, that great moment of redemption, when God rescued his people from the chaos of Egypt and led them toward a new life of shalom in the Promised Land.

Then God's judgment fell. The Hebrews watched all through that terrible night as the death angel passed over Egypt. Not one house in Egypt was spared. But God protected every household that had been marked with the blood of the Passover lamb. Before the night was over, Pharaoh told the Hebrews to leave and the Egyptians urged them to hurry. Thus the Hebrews left Egypt as free people.

But what did their freedom mean? It is not easy for people who have lived in bondage to live, think, and act like free persons. The bigger issue of slavery was not who "owned" them but to whom they "belonged" as a result of their own desires and choices. Unless the Hebrews made the life-changing, passionate commitment to follow the God who loved and saved them, they would remain slaves to the "Egypt within," to a more wretched spiritual bondage than the physical slavery they had experienced in Egypt.

As the Israelites left Egypt behind, God continued their "basic training" so that they would discover their calling, be obedient to his purpose, and experience the shalom of true freedom. That training actually began before the tenth plague, when God issued the Passover commands. It intensified after they walked into the desert.

# Opening Thoughts (3 minutes)

*The Very Words of God*

> *Because GOD kept watch, all Israel for all generations will honor GOD by keeping watch this night.*

*Exodus 12:42 (The Message)*

### Think About It

When we find ourselves in a difficult situation, or when we face unknown challenges that involve high risk or uncertainty, we have a choice to make. We may know that we need to call out to God in faith and "watch" as he guides and protects us one step at a time, but we will often start evaluating our options and planning strategies in an effort to handle things on our own.

How do you think God trains us to walk with him rather than on our own? What do you think are God's "basic training" requirements to ensure that those who are partners in his story trust him fully and obey everything he says?

# DVD Notes (29 minutes)

**Set free—for training to *be* God's message**

**Trapped by the sea, but not alone**

**A night of watching: God watches, Israel watches**

**Steps of faith to follow the Shepherd's call**

## DVD Discussion (6 minutes)

1.  Imagine the atmosphere when the Israelites left Egypt. Look at the map on the facing page showing the various routes from Egypt to the Promised Land. Depending on which route they took, how far would they have to travel? How long do you think it would take? What do you think they expected the journey to the Promised Land to be like?

    Do you think they had any idea that they would need "training" to become God's people who would help restore his shalom to the world? Why or why not?

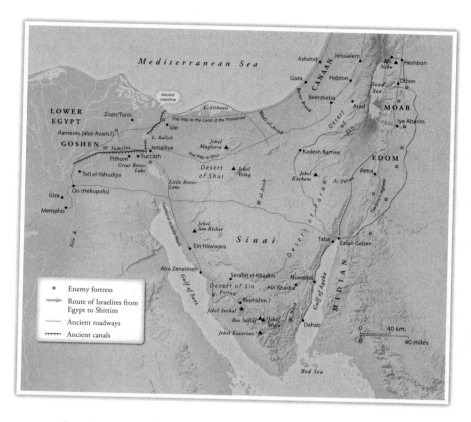

In what ways do you think the Israelites' idea of what they needed differed from God's idea?

2.  As the Israelites camped between the sea and the chariots of Pharaoh's army, what do you think they felt and thought about during that long night of watching?

In what way(s) was this night similar to or different from that recent night of watching when God had protected them as the angel of death passed over their doorposts?

3. In light of God's promises to the Israelites, revealed to them by Moses while they were still slaves, why was it significant that they called out to God *by name*?

What does this indicate about who they were becoming?

How much do you imagine they thought about God's promises that night? Why?

## Small Group Bible Discovery and Discussion (15 minutes)

*Time to Leave: God Ushers In a New Beginning*

Before sending the final "Passover" plague — one of the most stunning events in his work of redeeming his broken world — God began molding and shaping the Hebrews into a faithful people who would love, follow, and obey him. He commanded them to do things they had never done before, things that could result in repercussions from the Egyptians, things for which they may not have understood the reason at the time. Great consequences hung in the balance.

Would they choose the God of their ancestors, or would they hold onto the gods of Egypt and the way of life they had always known?

1.  Apart from Moses and Aaron, the text barely mentions the Hebrews during the first nine plagues. In what context are they mentioned, and what distinction between Egyptians and Hebrews did God make? (See Exodus 8:19 – 23; 9:4, 26; 10:23; 11:4 – 7.)

    Why do you think God made this distinction at this time?

    What do you think that distinction may have meant to the Hebrews, and to Pharaoh and the Egyptians?

2.  Through the exodus experience, God was creating something new with his people. This wasn't a "clean up the outside" newness; it was a fundamental change in belief, worldview, and way of life. Consider some of the basic elements of perception and lifestyle that God changed.

    a.  The Egyptian calendar — the number of months, length of weeks, and designation of seasons — was constructed around the gods of Egypt. What fundamental change did God command even before the tenth plague began, and what, by implication, did God want the Hebrews to renounce completely? (See Exodus 12:1 – 2; 20:3 – 5.)

b.   The Egyptians had a twelve-month solar calendar, and
they worshiped the sun. On what did God begin and end
the months in the Hebrews' calendar, and in what ways
might this have helped to break their reliance on the
Egyptian worldview? (See Numbers 10:10; 28:14.)

## PROFILE OF A CULTURE
### Two Calendars, Two Worldviews

The Egyptians carved their calendar in stone virtually everywhere. They used
a twelve-month solar calendar of 365 days (quite similar to the one we use
today!) that began with the annual Nile flood (inundation) as the star Sopdet
(Sirius) rose. Each month comprised thirty days, divided into ten-day weeks.
Each week was devoted to worship of one Egyptian god. After 360 days (at
the time of low water), they celebrated the birthdays of Osiris, Seth, Isis,
Nephthys, and Horus for five days. This was a time to worship and implore
the gods to provide a blessed inundation and an abundant harvest (ma'at, or
harmony and order, in their world). So even the calendar perpetuated Egypt's
story and worldview in daily life.

In contrast, God established a calendar for the Hebrews that represented
his story and worldview. Just as he had created the universe, he was now
creating a new people. So God instituted a seven-day week to remind them
that he had created the world in six days and rested on the seventh day
(Genesis 1:31; 2:1–3), and he designated that each year begin with the
celebration of Passover (Exodus 12:1–3) to represent their redemption from
slavery. The calendar year ended with the celebration of Sukkoth, a festival
designed to recall the time in the desert when God molded and shaped them
into his people. For Israel, each year of life began and ended by recalling
their redemption from Egypt. After seven cycles of seven years (on the fiftieth
year), God commanded that Israel celebrate Jubilee by setting free all those

in the bondage of indentured servanthood or debt. The reason for this act of restoration was because God had set the Hebrews free from Egypt (Leviticus 25:10, 35–42, 54–55). God's view of restoration and shalom practiced in daily life is perpetuated through the calendar he established.

3.  God chooses human partners in bringing about his work of redemption, but they cannot accomplish his work if they persist in following the world's way of chaos rather than his way of shalom. So, faithful obedience to God in everything is essential. For the Hebrews, preparation for the Passover was their first big lesson in how to obey God faithfully. (See Exodus 12:3 – 14, 24 – 28.)

    a.  Which specific actions did God command of the Hebrews, and what would be the consequences if they did not obey him?

    b.  For what reason(s) do you think God gave such specific instructions?

    c.  As God began retraining his people, what did he have Moses tell them to remember at the start of each year for the rest of history, and what was their response? Were they starting to get the message? Why or why not?

## Faith Lesson (6 minutes)

For the Israelites, there is a sense in which time began with the exodus, and this new beginning was reflected in God's establishment of their new calendar. Although this change may not seem significant to us, consider how a calendar sets the rhythm of life. It shapes our work, our leisure, our worship, our remembrance of the past. A new calendar put into process a new basis for how the Israelites were to view and live life.

1. What do you think it meant for the Israelites to live with a sense that time began with the exodus, and how do you think that experience affected their daily life and relationship with God?

2. As Christians, our identity is based on the death and resurrection of Jesus. His sacrifice as the Lamb of God, which actually took place on Passover, is the redemptive "exodus" that led to our freedom from bondage to sin and chaos. If you are a follower of Jesus, in what ways might you live more passionately, obediently, and gratefully if you focused on the great beginning that led you into a new identity in partnership with God?

   To what extent do Jesus' great redemptive acts — birth, death, resurrection — organize your time and the rhythm of your life?

What things could you do (on a daily basis as well as an annual basis) to root more of your life in Jesus' acts of redemption that have set you free from sin?

3. Today, like the ancient Hebrews, we also must recognize when it is time to leave behind not only a life of chaos but every reminder of chaos that may hold us in bondage. In which area(s) of your life is it "time to leave Egypt"?

What does your personal calendar — past, present, and current activities, goals, plans — reveal about where you place your real identity and commitment?

In what ways is it time for you to take a bold stand and get rid of your "old calendar"?

What changes will you make on your personal calendar in an effort to "leave behind" the world of chaos and live each day as a gift from God in which you have been set free from sin's bondage to live by the freedom of obedience to his Word?

## Closing (1 minute)

Read together Proverbs 3:5 – 7: "Trust in the LORD with all your heart and lean not on your own understanding; in all your ways acknowledge him, and he will make your paths straight. Do not be wise in your own eyes; fear the LORD and shun evil."

Then pray, thanking God for his great acts of redemption that truly set us free from chaos. Ask God to soften your heart and mind so you will be more sensitive to the leading of his Word. Ask for the wisdom to trust him even when you do not know where he is leading you. Ask him for the strength to "walk with him" every moment of every day and reflect him to the watching world.

## Memorize

> *Trust in the LORD with all your heart and lean not on your own understanding; in all your ways acknowledge him, and he will make your paths straight. Do not be wise in your own eyes; fear the LORD and shun evil.*

*Proverbs 3:5 – 7*

# Choosing God's Story

*In-Depth Personal Study Sessions*

## Day One | God Chooses the Exodus Route

### The Very Words of God

> *When Pharaoh let the people go, God did not lead them on the road*
> *through the Philistine country, though that was shorter. For God said,*
> *"If they face war, they might change their minds and return to Egypt."*
> *So God led the people around by the desert road toward the Red Sea.*

> *Exodus 13:17 – 18*

### Bible Discovery

### *God Leads His People Like a Shepherd*

No doubt the Hebrews in Egypt had heard of God's promises concerning the Promised Land (Genesis 12:1 – 3; 26:1 – 3), but none of them had been there. So they must have left Egypt with an intense sense of anticipation, excitement, and perhaps some apprehension as well. They were no longer slaves, but the Egyptians were driving them out of the only land, culture, and occupations they had ever known. As they walked toward the desert east of Goshen and passed by Egyptians who were still burying their firstborn, they must have been amazed by their God's mighty power. But what did the future hold for them? Most of what they knew about gods related to the natural world of the Nile — gods for the annual inundation, gods of frogs and crocodiles, gods for fertility of crops and family, gods of creation and seasons, and many more. Who exactly was the God who had set them free? Would he go with them into the desert, and would he be as powerful there as he had been in Egypt?

1. Where did the Israelites think they were going? (See Exodus 3:8; 6:2 – 8.)

2. How long do you think the Israelites thought the journey would take? (See Exodus 3:18; 5:3; 8:27.)

## FOR GREATER UNDERSTANDING
### Where Was the Route from Egypt to the Sea?

The Torah clearly and precisely describes the exodus from Egypt, and this study accepts the story provided in the Torah as completely accurate. But despite the Bible's precision, many historical and geographical questions concerning the exodus remain unanswered. We know the names of cities and places along the Israelites' route to the sea, but we don't know where each location is. We know Ra'amses is where they started out, but where are Pithom, Succoth, Etham, Pi-hahiroth, Migdol, and Baal Zephon, the places the Bible mentions as they neared the sea? Which sea did they cross? Which Pharaoh was the Pharaoh of the exodus?

Such questions have long intrigued Bible students. Although the Bible gives many clues and hints as to specific places, routes, and people, it doesn't give enough data for us to arrive at definitive answers. The best answers we have, then, are theories based on the biblical story that are supported by one scientific conclusion or another.

Fortunately, this study does not depend on our knowing all of the specific locations and routes. Our emphasis is best expressed by the Middle Eastern saying, "It is not where an event occurred that is important but where it is remembered." Whereas knowing a specific setting for a biblical story often enhances and enriches our understanding, the text itself provides the lesson. Therefore, the locations filmed for this study are *representative* of places where the story occurred and are similar to the Torah's descriptions. No attempt has been made to "prove" that these are the actual places.

3. As the Hebrews left Egypt, who joined them? (See Exodus 12:37 – 38.)

   What does this suggest about the effect that God's gift of freedom from bondage can have on other people?

   On animals as part of God's creation?

4. What two distinct parts (or phases) of the Israelites' journey does God identify? (See Exodus 3:8; 6:6 – 8.)

   From God's perspective, what do you think was important about each part of the journey?

   To what extent do you think the Israelites were aware that this was a two-part journey or that it would require more of them than just moving from one place to another? Why?

5. Although the Israelites left Egypt boldly, thinking they were ready to fight whatever they might face, what did God, as their Shepherd, do to protect them during this early stage of their journey? (See Exodus 13:17 – 18.)

What indications were there, before the Israelites left Egypt, that they could become discouraged easily? (See Exodus 4:29 – 31; 6:6 – 9.)

What did the response of the Israelites to Pharaoh's pursuing army indicate about their readiness to be active participants in fulfilling their role in God's story? What if the army they faced had been the Philistines? (See Exodus 14:10 – 12.)

**THINK ABOUT IT**

Was concern that the Israelites might go back to Egypt the only reason God did not lead them through Philistine territory immediately after they left Egypt (Exodus 13:17)? God easily could have dealt with the Philistines; he had just overwhelmed the world's most powerful empire. Certainly he could have fought for the Israelites again. What really was at stake? What does God's statement that they would be afraid of the Philistines tell you about the Israelites? What did God desire more than simply moving his people back to the land of their ancestors?

If God had allowed the Israelites to take the short route to Canaan, what would they have missed? (For some ideas, consider Exodus 16:10 – 31; 24:1 – 11; 34:29 – 35; 39:32 – 40:38.) What did God have to do to not only bring them "out" of Egypt but "into" the Promised Land? What had to change in their character and identity for them to step into their new role as God's partners in the Promised Land (Joshua 24:14 – 15)? Why would you expect these changes to take longer than a few weeks?

## Reflection

No matter how indirect or long the route was that the Israelites took from Egypt to the Promised Land, it was exactly the route God had prepared for them: "There will be a highway for the remnant of his people . . . as there was for Israel when they came up from Egypt" (Isaiah 11:16). God apparently was preparing the Israelites to do more than sit on the sidelines and watch him in action. As they started walking out of Egypt, God seems to have been teaching, guiding, and preparing them to go into the Promised Land as his partner in bringing shalom to all things.

Because he dearly loved his chosen people, God refused to use the shortcut they no doubt would have preferred. Because of the training they needed in order to build faith and flee fear, he chose a much longer and more difficult way. As God told Moses to say to Israel: "You yourselves have seen what I did to Egypt, and how I carried you on eagles' wings and brought you to myself. Now if you obey me fully and keep my covenant, then out of all nations you will be my treasured possession. Although the whole earth is mine, you will be for me a kingdom of priests and a holy nation" (Exodus 19:4 – 6).

How important was God's purpose for his people — teaching, guiding, preparing them as his partners — through the exodus?

How does God's purpose for the exodus help you to understand why God sometimes guides his beloved people today to take more difficult paths rather than shortcuts?

What do God's dealings with his people through the exodus suggest to you about his reasons for leading you on the path you are on?

When they left Egypt, the Hebrews probably had little, if any, idea of how difficult their journey to Canaan would be. When has God led you to take steps of faith when you had no idea how difficult things would become?

In what way(s) has God used a path much tougher than you expected to teach you something important?

What did you learn on the extended journey that you would have missed if you had taken the "shortcut"?

Where do you think you are on your journey? Are you still sitting back, watching God act with great power (if so, why?), or is it time for you to start taking action?

How does the fact that God faithfully watches over his people help you to face uncertain or really tough times on your journey?

What might be the purpose(s) for which God allows or even chooses a difficult path for you?

## Memorize

*I run in the path of your commands, for you have set my heart free. Teach me, O LORD, to follow your decrees; then I will keep them to the end. Give me understanding, and I will keep your law and obey it with all my heart. Direct me in the path of your commands, for there I find delight.*

*Psalm 119:32–35*

# Day Two | Trapped Against the Sea

## The Very Words of God

*Then the LORD said to Moses, "Tell the Israelites to turn back and encamp near Pi Hahiroth, between Migdol and the sea. They are to encamp by the sea, directly opposite Baal Zephon."*

*Exodus 14:1–2*

## Bible Discovery

### *Where Would God's People Turn for Help?*

If the Hebrews had any doubt about whether or not their God was more powerful than the Egyptian gods, their uncertainty ended when the angel of death passed over Egypt and claimed the lives of Egypt's firstborns. Protected by God through their faith in placing the lambs' blood on their doorposts, the Hebrews were spared and set free. As these awestruck, former slaves started walking out of Egypt during the early morning hours, the Egyptians showered them with riches. Surely God had redeemed them! No Israelite who had experienced that night would ever forget it! Three days later, however, these same people faced a new threat. Once again they had to choose whether or not they would trust in their God to be with them as he had promised.

1.  The Hebrews had been immersed in Egypt's culture for so long that it seems they needed a "refresher course" in knowing their God. The plagues certainly played a role in helping

them rediscover the mighty God of Israel. Shortly before
they started walking out of Egypt, which steps had God
asked the Israelites to take in order to act upon their belief
and faith in him? (See Exodus 12:1 – 42.)

| Preparing for the Exodus | Steps of Faith the Israelites Took |
|---|---|
| Ex. 12:3 – 5 | |
| Ex. 12:6 | |
| Ex. 12:7 | |
| Ex. 12:8 – 10 | |
| Ex. 12:11 | |
| Ex. 12:33 – 37 | |

2. While the Israelites walked along the desert road and
   camped by the sea, what evidence did they see of God's
   faithful presence and leading? (See Exodus 13:18, 21 – 22;
   14:19 – 20.)

What do you think these visible signs meant to them?

Why would these signs have been important for people who were used to being slaves and still had a lot to learn about their God and his love and faithfulness?

3. As part of his ongoing "basic training" for his chosen people, what seemingly illogical (from a human perspective) command did God give to the Israelites? (See Exodus 14:1 – 4.)

   If you had been an Israelite, what might you have thought about this apparent change in plans?

   How did the Israelites respond, and what does this reveal about their faith in God and in Moses, his messenger?

4. When Pharaoh learned of the Israelites' whereabouts, what did he decide to do, and why? (See Exodus 14:5 – 9.)

## PROFILE OF A CULTURE

### The Egyptian Chariot

At the time the Israelites left Egypt for the Promised Land, the Egyptian Empire boasted the world's most powerful and well-equipped army. Egypt's chariot forces were the foundation around which the Egyptian army was built. Chariot units moved together to protect foot soldiers from advancing enemy troops, to attack an enemy's flank and create chaos, or to charge enemy chariots in a well-spaced line abreast.

Valued for speed rather than armor, an open-backed Egyptian chariot was built of a bent wood frame and lightweight wicker material placed over an axle and two wheels. Egyptian chariots were lighter and more maneuverable

**EGYPTIAN-STYLE CHARIOTS, WHICH WERE PULLED BY TWO HORSES AND MANNED BY A DRIVER AND A WARRIOR, RACE ACROSS THE DESERT.**

**A MODERN RECONSTRUCTION OF AN EGYPTIAN CHARIOT**

than the chariots of other powers such as the Hittites. The rapid acceleration and shorter turning radius of Egyptian chariots enabled Egypt's army to penetrate enemy lines and trap enemy forces between its chariots and infantry. No wonder seeing and hearing the rapid approach of Pharaoh's elite chariot unit — and every other chariot in Egypt — struck terror into the hearts and minds of the Israelites!

5. While camped between the sea and Pharaoh's approaching army, how did the Israelites respond when they saw the Egyptian army coming? (See Exodus 14:10 – 12; compare to Exodus 2:23.)

What were they slowly learning about being committed to God and allowing him to shape them?

Do you think they felt abandoned by God in this situation? Why or why not?

How much of the "good life" in Egypt was still a part of the Israelites' thinking despite all of the suffering they had experienced there?

## PROFILE OF A CULTURE
### Egypt's Obsession with Death

From the Valley of the Kings to the Great Pyramids of Giza, from Tutankhamen's tomb to the workers' tombs, no culture has emphasized death, burial, and the afterlife quite like the Egyptians. Structures like pyramids, funerary temples, and tombs functioned as a kind of sacred text for the Egyptians, who portrayed their theology in carved stone. Thousands of the world's most elaborate tombs are located in Egypt.

**THE PYRAMID OF KHAFRE AT GIZA WAS A THOUSAND YEARS OLD WHEN GOD BROUGHT THE HEBREWS OUT OF EGYPT. CONTAINING MORE THAN TWO MILLION BLOCKS AT ITS CORE, THIS STUNNING PYRAMID WAS ORIGINALLY COVERED IN FINE-DRESSED LIMESTONE, MUCH OF WHICH HAS BEEN PLUNDERED FOR USE IN LATER BUILDING PROJECTS.**

It would have been impossible to live in ancient Egypt and not know how important a role death played in the culture. So consider the sarcasm of the trapped Israelites when, as the Egyptian army approached, they cried out to Moses, "Was it because there were no graves in Egypt that you brought us to the desert to die?" (Exodus 14:11). Of course there were graves in Egypt! Everyone knew Egypt had an abundance of tombs.

6.  For what three purposes does the text say God placed the Israelites in such a threatening situation? (See Exodus 14:4, 13 – 14.)

How are God's purposes in this situation similar to what he had been doing all along?

There is a saying that goes, "We never learn that God is all we need until God is all we've got." In what ways is that an expression of God's purpose in allowing the Israelites to be trapped between Pharaoh's chariots and the sea?

## Reflection

Today God still molds and shapes his people just as he did the Israelites. He knows what he desires his people to become, and he knows what it will take to train them in his ways. Whether the circumstances he uses to accomplish his purposes are comfortable, uncomfortable, or even painful, he remains loving, patient, and faithful. And he will be there to act with power and deliver his people when they need him to fight for them.

During the darkest hours of the Israelites' vigil by the sea, the text says, "Then the angel of God, who had been traveling in front of Israel's army, withdrew and went behind them. The pillar of cloud also moved from in front and stood behind them, coming between the armies of Egypt and Israel" (Exodus

14:19 – 20). What comfort, peace, and hope do you think this provided for the Israelites?

How does the fact that God faithfully watches over his people help you to face tough times?

When have you experienced a powerful sign of God's faithfulness in the midst of a difficult situation?

What did it mean to you at the time?

What does it mean to you now?

How important is it to pass on this example of God's faithfulness to others who may be experiencing difficult challenges?

Could it be that God still places his people in tough circumstances to teach us that we can trust him completely *and* to bring glory to his name? Why or why not?

What might some of those circumstances be?


When you face a situation in which it seems there is no way out, how do you respond?


What do you think God wants you to learn about calling out to him in faith, trusting in him, and waiting for his deliverance?


What do you think God wants you to learn about the way you try to handle things on your own?


What do you think God wants you to realize about the seductive pull your "Egypt" exerts on you that draws you away from him and his promises?


## Memorize

*Moses answered the people, "Do not be afraid. Stand firm and you will see the deliverance the LORD will bring you today. The Egyptians you see today you will never see again. The LORD will fight for you; you need only to be still."*

*Exodus 14:13 – 14*

## Day Three | God's Incredible Promises

### The Very Words of God

> *Therefore, say to the Israelites: "I am the* Lord, *and I will bring you out from under the yoke of the Egyptians. I will free you from being slaves to them, and I will redeem you with an outstretched arm and with mighty acts of judgment. I will take you as my own people, and I will be your God."*

*Exodus 6:6 – 7*

### Bible Discovery

### *Four Promises of Redemption*

Immediately after Moses and Aaron obeyed God and confronted Pharaoh, the condition of the enslaved Hebrews worsened. This turn of events troubled Moses. It seemed to him that God had not rescued his people at all, so he asked God why. God explained his plan and promised to do four specific things for the Israelites. According to some Jewish traditions, these four promises are the progressive stages of the Hebrews' redemption from slavery in Egypt. As you explore these promises, consider all that God's redemption involves.

1.  When Moses questioned God about the trouble his people faced in Egypt, God prefaced his answer with a reminder of Israel's history. Which relationships did God bring to Moses' mind? (See Exodus 6:2 – 5.)


    Considering the following passages, why do you think each relationship God brought to mind was important in light of what he was preparing to do for his enslaved people in Egypt?

    Genesis 12:1 – 3


    Genesis 15:12 – 14

Genesis 26:23 – 25

Genesis 28:10 – 15

Genesis 46:2 – 4

2.  In response to Moses' concern regarding what God would do for the Israelites, what promises did God make before the plagues began? Write down each one, and notice how the fulfillment of the promise would redeem God's people. (See Exodus 6:6 – 7.)

| The Promise | How God Would Redeem His People |
|---|---|
| 1: | He would set them free and end their brutal suffering. |
| 2: | He would change their very nature so they would be free of "slave" thinking. |
| 3: | He would remove the stains of slavery and attachment to Egypt and its gods so the Hebrews would be forgiven and clean. |
| 4: | He would set them apart as his own people and would be bound to them forever as their protector and leader. |

## DID YOU KNOW?

These four promises—to bring out, to free, to redeem, and to take—are recalled in the ritual of the four cups of wine during every Jewish Passover Seder. This practice was apparently established by the time of Jesus, as the Gospels mention Jesus taking the cup during the Passover meal with his disciples. For which cup might Jesus have given thanks in Luke 22:17–18?

## FOR GREATER UNDERSTANDING
### What Does Redemption Mean?

In biblical tradition, a redeemer intervenes on behalf of an indebted or enslaved relative by paying a ransom to gain redemption or release. Any past debt or failure that led to the bondage is considered paid in full, so the redeemed person is, in a sense, forgiven and clean. The Hebrew Scriptures record many examples of redemption, such as God redeeming the Hebrews (Exodus 6:6; 1 Chronicles 17:21); redemption of property (Leviticus 25:25–28; Ruth 4:2–5); and redemption from sin (Psalm 130:7–8; Titus 2:11–14).

When Jesus said, "This is my blood of the covenant, which is poured out for many for the forgiveness of sins" (Matthew 26:28), he was describing how his atoning death would "purchase" or redeem us to set us free from slavery to sin and death (Romans 6:6, 22–23). By this transaction of his shed blood, Jesus, the sacrificial Lamb of God, has redeemed all people who have invited him by faith to be Lord and Savior of their lives (John 3:16; Ephesians 2:8–9).

Jesus' disciples understood the magnitude of his redemptive "purchase" of humankind. The apostle Peter wrote, "For you know that it was not with per-ishable things such as silver or gold that you were redeemed from the empty way of life handed down to you from your forefathers, but with the precious blood of Christ, a lamb without blemish or defect" (1 Peter 1:18–19). As Christians, we have been set free from being slaves to sin (Galatians 5:1). Like the Hebrews, whose obedience demonstrated an act of belief and faith in God, we place our belief and faith in Jesus when we receive his salvation. Our sins have been forgiven, we have been made clean (1 John 1:9), and God will preserve us as his own.

## Reflection

There is a Jewish belief that sometimes the Scriptures record only God's part of a conversation between him and his people or that the text is God's response to what his people are thinking. There is a rabbinic midrash based on Exodus 6:6–7 that shows what the Hebrews may have been thinking. Although only God's part of the conversation is actually part of the Scripture, the midrash provides a perspective that may help us to better understand our own redemption.

HEBREWS: We are slaves to the powerful Egyptians. We will never be free!

GOD'S MESSAGE: I will bring you out from under the yoke of the Egyptians.

HEBREWS: But once we are free, how will we live? We are slaves by nature and have never learned how to live free. We do not know how to act, for we are still slaves at heart. We still act like Egyptians.

GOD'S MESSAGE: I will free you from being slaves to them.

HEBREWS: But we have been polluted by our slavery in Egypt. We have worshiped their gods, and practiced their disobedient practices. We are an unclean people unworthy of you, our God.

GOD'S MESSAGE: I will redeem you.

HEBREWS: But what if we go back to Egypt? What if the Egyptians come after us to force us back to slavery?

GOD'S MESSAGE: I will take you as my own people, and I will be your God.

These four promises of God that Moses thundered to the Hebrews relate to everyone who needs redemption, including people today. Take time to make this midrash personal to you and your relationship with God. For each of God's four promises, on the next page write out your side of the conversation:

*Promise 1:* Of course you are not "under the yoke" of the Egyptians, but you still face things that can enslave you. What are they?

*Promise 2:* When it comes to joining God as his partner in restoring shalom to his creation, not one of us truly knows how to live. If we are honest, we often realize that we are more enslaved than we may want to admit. In what ways are you still a slave at heart?

*Promise 3:* When we catch a glimpse of who God really is and see the vision of his redemptive story, the ugliness of our sin is overwhelming. What has made you unclean?

*Promise 4:* All who desire to be God's partners in redemption have fears that we will fail to become the people God is training us to be. In what ways are you afraid that you will fail God?

## Day Four | An Issue of the Heart

### The Very Words of God

*The LORD hardened Pharaoh's heart, and he was not willing to let them go. Pharaoh said to Moses, "Get out of my sight! Make sure you do not appear before me again! The day you see my face you will die."*

***Exodus 10:27 – 28***

## Bible Discovery

### *Pharaoh's Hardened Heart*

Much has been discussed and written about the perplexing hardening of Pharaoh's heart in the story of the exodus. As the plagues progressed, the hardening of Pharaoh's heart sometimes is attributed to his choice and sometimes to God's action. *If God hardened Pharaoh's heart,* people wonder, *was Pharaoh responsible for his actions? Was Pharaoh guilty of wrongdoing, or was he manipulated by God?* When we engage in such discussion, it is helpful to consider the implications of this issue from the perspective of ancient Egypt. Although a "hardened heart" can simply be a metaphor for Pharaoh's stubborn attitude, the hardening of Pharaoh's heart in the exodus story played a central role in the conflict between the gods of Egypt (and that included Pharaoh, who was considered to be divine) and the God of the Hebrews.

1. When did God inform Moses that he would "harden" Pharaoh's heart? (See Exodus 4:19 – 21.)


   What would be the result of Pharaoh's hardened heart?


   Why do you think God deemed it important for Moses to know how Pharaoh would respond?

# DID YOU KNOW?

## Two Perspectives on a Hardened Heart[1]

The Hebrew Bible uses the word *heart* to describe a person's essential character—mind, will, morals, and feelings—the place where one's behavior is determined. The Hebrew language uses three words to describe Pharaoh's hardened heart:

- *Hazaq,* meaning "tough" or "strong" (Exodus 4:21; 9:12; 10:20, 27; 14:4, 8)
- *Qasa,* meaning "difficult" or "stubborn" (Exodus 7:3)
- *Kaved,* meaning "heavy" (Exodus 8:15, 32; 9:34; 10:1)

These words appear to be interchangeable in the exodus story and are usually translated as "harden/ed." So, whether by Pharaoh's choice or God's action, Pharaoh's heart became hard or stubborn. Based on the Hebrew words used, the text also suggests that Pharaoh's heart was *heavy,* and that had significant implications in light of Egyptian beliefs.

Like the Hebrews, the Egyptians considered the heart to be a person's central essence or inner self. The heart encompassed intellect, emotions, will, and character. According to an Egyptian sacred text, "The Book of the Dead," a person's heart was evaluated after death to determine his or her fate in the afterlife. Egyptians believed that during a person's earthly life, his or her heart either became "heavy" due to misdeeds or improper behavior or remained light because the person lived a proper life filled with good actions.

So what meaning would the Egyptians attach to a Pharaoh who had a heavy heart? That Pharaoh would not be perfect. He would be guilty of "misdeeds" or sins against the God of the Hebrews and thus would deserve the judgment of the plagues. If the God of the Hebrews succeeded in making Pharaoh's heart heavy, then he would be Pharaoh's judge and superior. It would imply that the God of the Hebrews, who had weighed Pharaoh's heart according to his standards, had found it to be "heavy."

2. Do you know how many times the hardening of Pharaoh's heart is mentioned in the story of the ten plagues? Take a fresh look at the story and take note of what is happening each time his heart is hardened. (See Exodus 4:21; 7:3, 13, 14, 22, 23; 8:15, 19, 32; 9:7, 12, 35; 10:1, 20, 27; 11:10; 14:4, 8, 17.)

a. In relationship to which plagues did Pharaoh harden his own heart, and in relationship to which ones did God harden Pharaoh's heart?

| The Plagues | Who Hardened Pharaoh's Heart? | The Text |
|---|---|---|
| Plague 1 — blood | | Ex. 7:22 |
| Plague 2 — frogs | | Ex. 8:15 |
| Plague 3 — gnats | | Ex. 8:19 |
| Plague 4 — flies | | Ex. 8:32 |
| Plague 5 — livestock | | Ex. 9:7 |
| Plague 6 — boils | | Ex. 9:12 |
| Plague 7 — hail | | Ex. 9:33 – 35 |
| Plague 8 — locusts | | Ex. 10:20 |
| Plague 9 — darkness | | Ex. 10:27 |
| Plague 10 — firstborn | | Ex. 11:10 |

b. How many times did God give Pharaoh a choice to obey him and let the Hebrews go or to harden his heart against God, and how patient was God with Pharaoh's choices?

c.  What was God revealing to the Egyptians by controlling Pharaoh's heart, and what impact did God's actions have? (See Exodus 9:10 – 10:7.)

3.  Why do you think Pharaoh, who was considered to be divine, was unmoved by the events of Exodus 8:16 – 19, which exposed the contest between the Egyptian gods and the God of the Hebrews?

Who realized they faced a greater power than anything they had known before, and why did they believe this?

## PROFILE OF A CULTURE
### Hope for the Afterlife

Much of the Egyptian culture focused on death and one's preparation for the afterlife. The name nineteenth-century scholars coined for the ancient Egyptian funerary text was "The Book of the Dead." Written on a papyrus scroll, this book was often placed in burial chambers or — in some elaborate buri-

**THE EGYPTIAN "BOOK OF THE DEAD"**

als—carved on tomb walls. As a sacred text, it had an extended description of the Egyptian concept of the afterlife. It served as a guidebook of behaviors to practice and behaviors to avoid, rituals, hymns, spells, and instructions to ensure that a deceased person would pass all obstacles to the afterlife.

The copy of the Egyptian funerary text shown on the previous page highlights elements that add meaning to the story of Pharaoh's "hard heart." At left, Anubis—god of the dead—brings the deceased person, Ani, to the scales of justice in the judgment hall. Anubis weighs Ani's heart (left scale) against a feather (right scale) symbolizing ma'at (harmony, or what is right). If the heart is weighted by misdeeds and is heavier than the feather, Amenit—the crocodile-headed god to the right of Anubis—devours Ani. If the heart is light, Ani is presented to Anubis, declared innocent of misdeeds, and ushered into the field of reeds—the paradise of the gods. Thoth, the ibis-headed god, keeps record of the proceedings before the jury of the gods above. As it turns out, Ani's heart is light, so Horus presents Ani to Osiris, Isis, and Nepthys (under the canopy on the right) as sinless.

All Egyptians except Pharaoh prepared for this judgment day by trying to live a moral life according to their standards, which included not offending any gods and preparing oneself with protective spells and chants and amulets that were placed in the tomb. Pharaoh, however, was believed to be the eternal incarnation of a god. He was believed to bring life and death, to be perfect according to Egyptian standards, and to have a "light" heart that was untainted by misdeeds. No one could contest his power or rule, and no one could judge him because he judged everyone else! His heart was always assumed to be equal to ma'at —as light as the feather that symbolized it.

4. What role did God intend humans to have in relationship to him, and in what sense did God give Pharaoh and the Egyptians an opportunity to participate in that relationship? (See Psalm 8; Hebrews 2:5 – 8.)

What does Exodus 14:4 add to your understanding of the exodus confrontation between God and the gods of Egypt?

What did God obtain by his judgment on the Egyptians, and what role did the hardening of Pharaoh's heart play in the process? (See Exodus 14:17 – 18.)

5.  All of us can choose to harden our hearts, but the Scriptures provide ample warning against the dangers of doing so. (See Psalm 95:6 – 11; Hebrews 3:12 – 15.)

    a.  What does a hardened heart indicate to God?

    b.  What is the penalty for a hardened heart?

    c.  What responsibility do Christians have to one another in relationship to the condition of their hearts?

## Reflection

God desires to restore shalom so that all people and all of creation will give glory to him (1 Corinthians 15:20 – 28; Ephesians 1:15 – 23). He cares a great deal about the condition of the human heart. A hard heart rejects the authority of God's lordship and proudly denies him the worship and glory he is due. A heart that seeks to know God and walk in his ways can partner with God to restore shalom to his world. Therefore, we always must be on guard to ensure that we do not follow in the hard-heartedness of Pharaoh.

What are some of the ways in which people today harden their hearts against God and obedience to his lordship as Pharaoh did?

When in your life has repeated resistance to God's ways led to a hardening of your heart toward God?

When God asks us to do something, why is it important for each of us to respond immediately rather than to resist him?

In what practical ways can you and others in your family and faith community encourage one another to have a pure, undivided, obedient heart before God?

In contrast to being hard-hearted, how will you bring glory to God today?

What will you do to help other people give him glory?

If we refuse to acknowledge him, might he still be glorified? Why or why not?

# Day Five | Keeping Watch with God

## The Very Words of God

*Because God kept watch, all Israel for all generations will honor God by keeping watch this night.*

*Exodus 12:42 (The Message)*

## Bible Discovery

### Nights of Watching

Imagine how the Israelites felt as midnight approached the night God had promised to unleash his tenth plague on the Egyptians. "I will pass through Egypt," God had said, "and strike down every first-born — both men and animals" (Exodus 12:12). So the Israelites had carefully obeyed God's instructions. They had put the blood of their Passover lambs on the doorposts so God's angel of death would pass

**THE HEBREWS PREPARE FOR THEIR NIGHT OF WATCHING.**

over their homes. They had packed their belongings and celebrated their deliverance with a hurried meal. Fully clothed and ready to leave, they gathered inside their homes, then watched and waited.

1.  According to Exodus 12:42, who was watching — keeping vigil — during the Passover night in Egypt?

    What did God command the Israelites to do forever in honor of his faithful, redemptive work that night?

2.  As the Israelites waited and watched again during another long night, this one by the sea, in what ways did God demonstrate that he was still "watching" over them? (See Exodus 14:10, 19 – 25.)

## FOR GREATER UNDERSTANDING
### Leyl Shimmurim

Jewish people still call the night after the Passover Seder *leyl Shimmurim,* meaning "night of watching" or "night of vigil." Just imagine what that night must have been like for the Hebrews. What did they think and feel during those emotionally laden hours in the dark of night? What did they anticipate a new life of freedom in the Promised Land to be? How excited or fearful were they about leaving the only way of life they had ever known? Did they wonder if the God of the universe whom they were getting to know (again) would

*continued on next page . . .*

keep his promises, and what it would be like to serve him? Did the wails of grief of their neighbors who had not placed lamb's blood on their doorposts cause them to fear Pharaoh's response?

As they waited, God also kept watch. Before the night was over, he fulfilled his promises of judgment against the Egyptians and freedom for his people. During the early morning hours, the Hebrews left Egypt as free people, but what would they do with their freedom?

Without a commitment to worship and know the God who freed them, the Hebrews would remain slaves to the Egypt within—to their own desires—and that would be a far more wretched slavery than the one they had left behind in Egypt. How would God continue training them to be partners in his story of redemption? How would he continue training them to walk in his ways and pursue his purpose—a training that had begun with their preparations before the tenth plague?

God commanded them to remember that they had watched all night and discovered that he also had watched over them. They were to keep remembering and honoring God for what he did—and they were to keep watching for his ongoing redemptive acts. He was not finished yet! There would be more "watching" over Israel, more protection, and more deliverance.

Just a few days after their long night of watching and waiting in Egypt, the Israelites faced another night of watching and waiting. This time they were trapped between Pharaoh's army and the sea. As Egyptian charioteers raced toward them, God's people had to choose their future: give up and serve the Egyptians again, or stand firm and watch for God's redemption.

They chose another night of watching. They began another vigil to see how God would watch over them as he had on Passover night. They watched as God's cloud moved to protect them from Pharaoh's army. They watched as the wind came up and divided the sea. They watched as God destroyed the army of Egypt. They had watched and waited, and knew that it was the Lord who had watched over them. For generations, even to this day, the Jewish people celebrate *leyl Shimmurim* in honor of the vigil God keeps to redeem his people.

3.  God gave specific instructions concerning the Hebrews'
    preparation for the tenth plague. Their obedience to his
    every command was essential to their survival.

    a.  What were God's instructions for the immediate situa-
        tion, and what would happen to anyone who was not
        under God's protection? (See Exodus 12:3 – 11.)

    b.  What resulted from the Hebrews' watching and their
        faithful obedience during those early morning hours?
        (See Exodus 11:1 – 3; 12:33 – 36.)

    c.  What were God's instructions for the future?

    | The Exodus Text | God's Instructions |
    |---|---|
    | 12:2, 14–20 | |
    | 12:24–27 | |
    | 13:3–10 | |

    d.  Why do you think God was making this event a founda-
        tional element in the lives of his people?

# FOR GREATER UNDERSTANDING
## Passing on a Spiritual Heritage

A culture leaves a lasting legacy by passing on its values, beliefs, and world-view to its children. The Egyptians passed on their culture through structures such as pyramids, temples, and palaces. In contrast, God instituted the Pass-over celebration as a way for his people to remember how he had set them free from the bondage they had known in Egypt and to protect and pass on the way of life he was entrusting to them. This annual ritual was more than an expression of gratitude to God; it was God's way of giving parents a sig-nificant experience through which they could explain their heritage and share their beliefs with their children.

To the Jews, Passover is much more than a recitation of events that hap-pened long ago. The story of Passover is the foundation of their very identity as God's redeemed people. So to celebrate Passover is to relive the events of their liberation from slavery in Egypt as if they had personally experienced it. They eat the unleavened bread of affliction and taste the bitter herbs of slavery. They drink the four cups of wine that symbolize the four promises of freedom. By participating in Passover, ancient history becomes reality.

For thousands of years, Jewish children have learned who they are by reliving the story of where they came from. They have learned that they belonged to a people who were rescued from slavery so that they (today) would cherish freedom. They belonged to a people who faced death so that they (today) would respect and defend life. They belonged to a people who were once slaves in a foreign land so that they (today) would not oppress the weak or ignore the stranger. Through the Passover, Jewish children become part of the story of God's people who have grown in character through many generations and are sustained by constantly remembering the story of their beginning that is still being written in their lives today.

4. God's vigil over his people did not end at Passover; it did not end at the crossing of the sea. For how long will God keep vigil over people who love (obey) him? (See Deuteronomy 7:9; Psalm 121:1 - 8.)

5. During Passover many years later, Jesus — the Lamb of God who would be sacrificed for the sins of all humanity — asked his disciples to keep watch with him. Review his interaction with them in Matthew 26:36 - 46 and Mark 14:32 - 42. What does Jesus' request, which he made following the Passover meal, indicate about the significance of what God was about to do?

Why do you think Jesus' disciples seem to have been so unaware of what was happening?

Do you think they had stopped "watching"? Why or why not?

## DID YOU KNOW?

### Passover as Part of Our Christian Identity

For followers of Jesus, the Passover story continues. The Messiah, our Passover Lamb (John 1:29; 1 Corinthians 5:7), was born to a people whose roots go back to the exodus and beyond. Their deliverance was one of God's many acts that contributed to the exact time and place of Jesus' birth. Nothing is more central to our deliverance from bondage to sin than the Messiah's redeeming death and resurrection.

The ancient Passover festival teaches us our own identity as people through whom God will make himself known to the world. The gospel accounts proclaim Jesus' saving work in terms of the Passover festival, which Jesus the Lamb of God came to complete. Through him, God established a new covenant sealed with his "blood." The Lord's Supper emerges from the feast before the night of watching. The blood of Jesus, shed on the same day as the exodus from Egypt was celebrated, rescues us from the bondage of sin and serves as the beginning of our journey with God.

Our very identity as God's people is rooted in exodus and Passover language. The more we know about the historical roots of that ancient festival, its rituals, and the Hebrews' understanding of it, the more profound will be our understanding of Jesus' life and ministry.

## Reflection

The nighttime "watching" events in the exodus experience of the ancient Hebrews provide insights into God's faithful care for his people and his ongoing work of redemption in the world. We too face difficult challenges and "long nights" when we must choose whether or not to trust the God who watches over everyone who obediently trusts in him.

> How passionately do you seek to obey God as the ancient Israelites did during their last night in Egypt and by the sea, and then watch for him to act?

The Israelites obeyed God's instructions even though it didn't make good sense to sacrifice lambs and paint their blood on the doorposts in a land where animal sacrifice was forbidden. How committed are you to obeying God even when it doesn't seem to make good sense?

In which area(s) of life do you face a difficult challenge for which you need God to watch over you and act powerfully on your behalf?

Do you trust him to be faithful and watch over you in this situation? Why or why not?

What have you done (or left undone) in preparation for him to act?

What does it mean for you to "stand vigil and wait" for him to act in this situation?

How do you respond to God when you have seen him act with great power to redeem his people?

Do you tell others what he has done? If yes, what is their response? If not, why not?

To what extent are you, and the community of God's people you know, passing on the heritage of God's faithfulness and deliverance — the original Passover, God's redemption through Jesus the Lamb, God's ongoing acts of redemption in the lives of people — to future generations?

Is this being done effectively in your family? In your church?

What will you, if you are a follower of Christ, do to more faithfully pass on the news of God's redeeming acts and encourage others to watch for God's "watching"?

## Memorize

*I lift up my eyes to the hills — where does my help come from?*
*My help comes from the Lord, the Maker of heaven and earth.*
*He will not let your foot slip — he who watches over you will not*
    *slumber;*
*indeed, he who watches over Israel will neither slumber nor sleep.*

**Psalm 121:1 – 4**

# THE LORD REIGNS: THE RED SEA

Imagine what it would have been like to stand on the eastern shore of the Red Sea with the ancient Hebrews and celebrate God's spectacular deliverance and proclaim his reign as Lord. So many things had changed in just a few days — from standing in the fertile farmland of Goshen to standing on a barren shoreline facing a mountainous desert; from being a slave defeated by Pharaoh's brutal demands to being set free by an awesome God who had utterly crushed Pharaoh's power; from having little to call your own to being laden down with the riches of Egypt; from living a seemingly hopeless existence to anticipating a new life in the Promised Land — it was almost too much to take in.

And that was just the beginning! The Hebrews' hearts had changed as well. They were no longer idol-worshiping slaves who cried out in anguish to no one in particular. They were free people who were beginning to know their God. Under God's training, they had risked Egypt's ire by killing year-old lambs and painting the blood on their doorposts. They had waited for God's chosen moment and followed Moses out of Egypt. They had followed the leading of the pillar of cloud and fire in the desert, even when they seemed to lead in the wrong direction.

Then, when Pharaoh's army thundered toward them, the Hebrews panicked but listened to the words of Moses and chose to trust the God of their ancestors. At God's command, Moses stretched out his arm. A great wind blew through the night, dividing the sea so that all of the Hebrews crossed through it on dry land. But the Egyptians were still in hot pursuit. At daybreak God told Moses to stretch out his arm again, and the Hebrews watched as the waters flowed back into place over the Egyptians. Not one survived.

What a stunning turn of events! Who could have imagined it? But what God had accomplished in the Hebrews' hearts and minds was no less dramatic and powerful than his redeeming acts in the crossing of the sea, and the Hebrews knew it. Standing safely on the far side of the sea, they rejoiced. In Eastern fashion, they danced and sang a praise-filled song about *their* sovereign, all-powerful, one-and-only God who had watched over them and redeemed them from Egypt. That day by the sea, the Hebrews — God's "firstborn son," Israel (Exodus 4:22) — made a faith commitment to the sovereign God who saved them.

As the Israelites danced and sang praises to the God who had redeemed them, they had no idea what a great journey they had just begun. From that point on, their lives and their culture would never be the same. Their commitment to God's lordship required them to participate obediently in his ongoing redemptive story. He had called them to bring shalom into the chaos of a sinful world, to be like him to other people, and to learn by his grace to obey his will.

The Jewish sages consider that day, when the Israelites danced on the shore of the sea and sang, "The Lord will reign forever and ever," to be the day the kingdom of heaven (i.e., kingdom of God) was born. Although the expression *kingdom of heaven* is not found in the Hebrew text (Old Testament), a kingdom exists whenever a king reigns. So as the Hebrews sang their commitment to the God who had delivered them, there was no uncertainty that he was their reigning King. By New Testament times, the idea of the *kingdom of heaven* was widely understood and taught in the Jewish world. It was the main theme of Jesus' teaching, and it was the message he assigned his disciples to pass on after his ascension.

The good news of God's kingdom that Jesus proclaimed was rooted in and shaped by the exodus experience. If we stand with the Israelites and seek to understand and celebrate their deliverance as they experienced it, we will appreciate more fully the grace-filled message and work of Jesus the Messiah. We also will be more responsive to the challenges, responsibilities, and privileges of being disciples of Jesus who are eager participants in God's amazing story and are committed to obey his will.

# Opening Thoughts (3 minutes)

## *The Very Words of God*

> *The LORD is my strength and my song; he has become my salvation.*
> *He is my God, and I will praise him, my father's God, and I will exalt*
> *him.... The LORD will reign for ever and ever.*

*Exodus 15:2, 18*

## Think About It

Many of us have seen God accomplish an amazing work in our lives or in the lives of people we know. Which experiences have had an impact on your life and your relationship with God?

In what ways have those experiences helped you to understand the difference between knowing *about* God — his attributes, his work of redemption, his commands — and *knowing* him as the sovereign Lord whom you trust, worship, and serve?

## DVD Notes (29 minutes)

**A changed people—*"This* is my God!"**

**The Lord will reign for ever and ever**

**The kingdom starts when God acts**

**Join the story**

## DVD Discussion (6 minutes)

1. Many people consider the crossing of the Red Sea to be the seminal event in God's shaping of his people. In what ways did the Israelites change between the time they left Egypt and when they stood on the other side of the sea after God divided the waters so that they could cross?

   What do you think caused the change?

2. When the waters of the Red Sea flowed back into place and Pharaoh's great army was no more, what was so significant about the Israelites singing, "*This* is my God"?

   What were they choosing, and what were they leaving behind?

3. When you realize that the song of Moses will be sung for eternity, and that the Israelites' offer of themselves as God's place to live is echoed in the event of Pentecost and in the apostle Paul's writings, what picture are you starting to see of God's story and how it unfolds throughout the Scriptures?

4.  What in the story of the Israelites' crossing the Red Sea
    causes you to get so excited that you want to sing and dance?

**NO MATTER WHERE THEY CROSSED THE SEA, THE ISRAELITES WOULD
HAVE ENCOUNTERED DESERT AND MOUNTAIN TERRAIN SIMILAR TO
THIS AREA OF THE EASTERN SHORE OF THE RED SEA.**

## Small Group Bible Discovery and Discussion (15 minutes)

### Israel Celebrates God as Their King

The "Song of the Sea," also called the "Song of Moses," is the first
biblical reference to a people recognizing God's reign as King in
their lives. The Israelites sang the song in celebration and praise of
*their* God, the God in whom they placed their trust after he rescued
them from Pharaoh's hand when they crossed the sea. Even today,
the song is recited in Jewish prayers and is viewed as a daily accep-

tance of God as King of the universe and a declaration of complete allegiance to him.

1. By now we have become quite familiar with God's miraculous intervention into human history that brought his people out of bondage in Egypt so that they could know their God and join as partners in his unfolding story. Theirs was not an easy journey, even to this point. As a group, review the story of the Hebrews' liberation from Egypt. Consider all that God did to enable his people to acknowledge him as their King and to celebrate his great power as they did on the shore of the sea. Write down what God has done — it will amaze you.

   a. What did God do in the life of Moses to redeem him and prepare him to be God's partner in leading the Hebrews out of bondage? (See Exodus 1:22 – 4:31.)

   b. What did God do to make himself known to Israel, Pharaoh, and the Egyptians through Moses and Aaron? List as many things as you can. (See Exodus 7:1 – 12:36.)

   c. What did God do to show the Israelites that he was with them and leading them as he had promised? (See Exodus 13:17 – 14:30.)

2.  Why do you think it took the Israelites so long to accept God
    as their Lord and King?

    What do you think finally convinced them that God was
    indeed *their* God who was worthy of honor, praise, and
    allegiance? Was it God's final act of judgment of Pharaoh
    and his army, his parting of the sea for the Israelites to cross,
    or a combination of all that had transpired since Moses
    went back to Egypt to deliver God's message? Explain your
    answer.

3.  Having finally recognized God's redemptive work on their
    behalf, how did the Israelites respond? (See Exodus 14:31;
    15:1 – 18, 21.)

    How do you respond to what God did? To what he is still
    doing today?

4. The Red Sea miracle became a central event in the identity of God's people. Generations after the crossing of the sea, what did the psalmist recognize about God as a result of what happened that night? (See Psalm 74:12 – 13.)

## FOR GREATER UNDERSTANDING
### Birth of a New Creation

In Egyptian mythology, a person who died would pass through a "sea of reeds" to be reborn and purified before entering paradise. There is a sense in which Judaism—perhaps influenced by what the Hebrews learned in Egypt or in recognition of the foundational nature of the crossing of the sea—also identifies the crossing of the "Reed" Sea as a new birth. The Hebrews entered the sea in bondage to Egypt's idols and came out of the sea as free people, in a sense a new creation, who could joyfully declare, "He (this) is my God" (Exodus 15:2)!

Another contributing factor to the crossing of the sea being viewed as a "new birth" is the fact that God used the wind (Hebrew: *ruach*, which also means "breath" or "spirit") to divide the water and bring a new people into existence. This echoes God's creation of the world when his Spirit—*ruach*—hovered over the waters and separated them to bring forth life (Genesis 1:1 – 10).

## Faith Lesson (6 minutes)

Having experienced God's miraculous acts of deliverance, the Israelites included these words in their "Song of the Sea:" "He is my God, and I will praise him, ... The LORD will reign for ever and ever" (Exodus 15:2, 18). They had left behind Egypt's gods and committed themselves to trust their God, the sovereign Creator of the universe, as their King. They offered themselves in submission to his reign in their lives and committed themselves to be the place where he lived!

1.  In what ways do you celebrate the greatness of God after he does a powerful work in your life or the life of a loved one?

    To what extent do you allow the joy of knowing him to come out through the "dance" of your heart — maybe even the dance of your feet?

    To what extent are you passionately committed to letting God reign in your life?

    NOTE: Recognizing that not everyone acknowledges God's sovereign reign, later Jewish sages spoke of people who would "enthrone" God in their lives by committing themselves to him as their King. Christian belief echoes the same thought. God is Lord over all, and those who "commit themselves to Jesus as their Lord and Savior" acknowledge, or "enthrone," him as Lord and accept his reign in their lives.

2.   When the Israelites sang and danced on the shore, there was no mistaking who they served. The evidence was obvious. What do you think is the evidence that a person in our world allows God to reign in his or her life?

How obvious is that evidence in your life?

When people who do not recognize God's lordship interact with you, what impact does the evidence of God's reign in your life have on them?

## Closing (1 minute)

Read together Revelation 4:11: "You are worthy, our Lord and God, to receive glory and honor and power, for you created all things, and by your will they were created and have their being."

Then pray, thanking God specifically for the great and wonderful things he has done to bring you into his story. Praise and celebrate him in prayer, and reaffirm your commitment to worship, love, and serve him as Lord and King.

### Memorize

*You are worthy, our Lord and God, to receive glory and honor and power, for you created all things, and by your will they were created and have their being.*

*Revelation 4:11*

# Choosing God's Story

*In-Depth Personal Study Sessions*

## Day One | God's Glory Reigns

### The Very Words of God

> *I will harden Pharaoh's heart, and he will pursue them. But I will gain*
> *glory for myself through Pharaoh and all his army, and the Egyptians*
> *will know that I am the LORD.*

> Exodus 14:4

### Bible Discovery

### *Another Intense Night of Watching*

As God continued to unfold his story of redemption, the Hebrews
became more active participants in it. When the time came for the
last plague, the one that would cause the Egyptians to drive them
out, the Hebrews chose to take action as God commanded. They
packed their belongings, killed the Passover lamb, painted its blood
on their doorposts, and asked their neighbors for silver and gold.
Then God led them out and they followed — not on the quick route
toward the Promised Land, but the long one. They followed when
God led them back toward Egypt and had them camp by the sea. But
was their God powerful enough and trustworthy to care for them
when their situation became desperate?

1.  After the Israelites left Egypt, Pharaoh changed his mind.
    He wanted his labor force back, so he assembled his chari-
    ots, horsemen, and troops and pursued the Israelites. He
    caught up with them as they camped by the sea. They were
    trapped, with no exit, and they were terrified. Imagine that
    you were one of them.

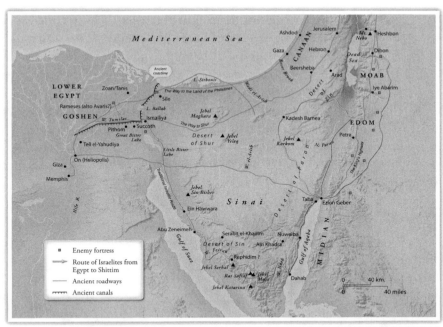

THE LOCATION WHERE THIS SESSION WAS FILMED IS NEAR THE
NORTHERN END OF THE GULF OF SUEZ, ON THE EASTERN SHORE OF
THE SEA WEST OF J. SIN BISHER. THIS SETTING IS SIMILAR TO WHAT
THE ISRAELITES WOULD HAVE ENCOUNTERED NO MATTER WHERE
THEY CROSSED THE SEA.

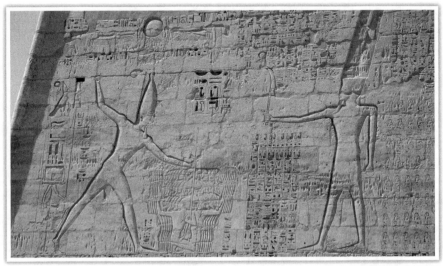

WITH THEIR BACKS AGAINST THE SEA, THE ISRAELITES
FACED THE WRATH AND RAISED ARM OF PHARAOH.

a.  Read the account of that night (Exodus 14:9 – 31) and
    write out what the Hebrews experienced. Write down
    the sights and sounds, the details and the contrasts, the
    emotions, the pace of events, the time of day. Try to
    imagine what you would have felt — physically, emotion-
    ally, and spiritually. Let this story, and what God accom-
    plished, come alive to you!

| Exodus Text | What the Hebrews Experienced |
|-------------|------------------------------|
| 14:9 – 10   |                              |
| 14:11 – 12  |                              |
| 14:13 – 14  |                              |
| 14:19 – 20  |                              |
| 14:21 – 22  |                              |
| 14:23       |                              |
| 14:24 – 25  |                              |
| 14:26 – 28  |                              |
| 14:29 – 31  |                              |

b.  Why do you think God orchestrated these events and
    performed these miracles in such a physically intense
    way?

c.  What impact did this experience have on his people?
    Why?

## DID YOU KNOW?
### Which "Sea" Did the Israelites Cross?

There is scholarly disagreement on exactly which body of water the Bible says the Israelites crossed. The word translated "Red Sea" in the English Bible is literally "Reed Sea" (in Hebrew, *Yam*: "sea" and *Suph*: "reed" or "papyrus") in the ancient Hebrew text. The Septuagint, the Greek translation of the Hebrew text undertaken by Jewish scholars circa 250 BC, called it the "Red Sea," and that identity has been passed on to the present.

Some scholars believe *Yam Suph* refers to the entire Red Sea mentioned in other Bible passages (1 Kings 9:26) and, therefore, is the name by which people in biblical times identified it. Other scholars conclude that the sea God divided is not the "Red Sea," which we call the Gulf of Suez, but the large, deep lakes between the Gulf of Suez and the Mediterranean. Both theories have been argued credibly. As always, the purpose of this study is not to advance any one argument about exodus-related geographical or historical settings except where the Bible is definitive. Our interest lies in what we can learn from the exodus story based on its ancient context.

2. The experience of the Israelites at the crossing of the Red Sea became a central event in their identity and a powerful testimony to later generations. What do you learn from the following passages about the long-term impact of that transformational night?

   Deuteronomy 11:2 – 4, 7 – 9

   Joshua 2:8 – 12; 24:6 – 7

   Psalm 66:5 – 7

Psalm 77:13 – 15, 19 – 20; 78:52 – 53


Psalm 106:7 – 12


Isaiah 43:15 – 19


## Reflection

What God accomplished through the crossing of the sea is well-known, even among people who do not follow the God of the Bible and may not even believe this event actually happened. But the miracles of the crossing and the work God accomplished in his people were powerful displays of his glory that have stood the test of time. They still relate to our lives today.

God certainly could have quietly destroyed Pharaoh and the Egyptian army in order to save his people, but he chose a different way. What do you think he wanted his people to experience through his spectacular display of power and glory?


How did the act of walking through the sea show their faith in God?


How does what God did that night apply to your understanding of faith and your view of God's character?

In what way(s) did you identify with what the Hebrews felt and how they acted during this long night?

How might it be beneficial to identify with them and view this night as part of *your* history too?

When you are in "deep water," how easily do you place your trust in God?

In what way might the experience of the Israelites in crossing the Red Sea influence how you respond the next time "your back is against the sea" and your only salvation lies in God?

## Memorize

*The enemy boasted, "I will pursue, I will overtake them. I will divide the spoils; I will gorge myself on them. I will draw my sword and my hand will destroy them." But you blew with your breath, and the sea covered them. They sank like lead in the mighty waters. "Who among the gods is like you, O Lord? Who is like you — majestic in holiness, awesome in glory, working wonders?"*

*Exodus 15:9 – 11*

## Day Two | God Destroys Pharaoh and His Gods

### The Very Words of God

*Moses stretched out his hand over the sea, and at daybreak the sea went back to its place. The Egyptians were fleeing toward it, and the* Lord *swept them into the sea. The water flowed back and covered the chariots and horsemen — the entire army of Pharaoh that had followed the Israelites into the sea. Not one of them survived.*

*Exodus 14:27 – 28*

### Bible Discovery

### *The Final Confrontation*

It's hard for us to imagine the power of ancient Egypt. We see ruins of amazing temples, pyramids, and other evidence of a great civilization, but to actually understand and feel the impact of that power in the everyday lives of people of that time is a whole different matter. We may be able to picture half a dozen chariots racing across the desert, for example, but one hundred times that many? That would require 1,200 horses! Try to imagine the reverence, fear, and awe that people felt toward Pharaoh, who was viewed as the one person who kept Egypt safe, fed, and prosperous. Try to imagine how Pharaoh himself felt as the God of the Hebrews defeated Egypt's gods and turned his entire worldview upside down. Perhaps it isn't all that surprising that Pharaoh tried one more time to challenge the God of the Hebrews in an attempt to defeat a little bit of chaos and reclaim some of what he had lost.

1.   Having experienced what God did through the ten plagues, how did Pharaoh and the Egyptians respond after the Hebrews left Egypt? (See Exodus 14:5 – 8.)

What had Moses' father-in-law concluded because of what God had done through the plagues that Pharaoh still did not seem to comprehend? (See Exodus 18:9 – 11.)

Why do you think it would have been so difficult for Pharaoh to believe that the God of the Hebrews was greater than he was and greater than the gods of Egypt?

Do you think Pharaoh thought he had anything left to lose by pursuing the Israelites? Why or why not?

## DID YOU KNOW?

### The East Wind

The east wind, called *kadim* in Hebrew, is a hot, dry, scorching wind. Such winds are known today as sirocco or *khamsin* (Arabic). As an instrument in God's hands, an east wind symbolized his judgment.

2. What kind of wind did God use to create a path through the sea, and what would this have meant to the Hebrews? (See Exodus 14:21.)

What does an east wind often symbolize in the Bible? (See Isaiah 27:8; Jeremiah 18:17; Jonah 4:6 – 8.)

When had God used an east wind previously in his dealings with Pharaoh and the gods of Egypt, and what message did it communicate? (See Exodus 10:13.)

3.  What did Moses, who was called to be like God to Pharaoh, do again by the sea, just as he (and Aaron) had done to bring the plagues upon Egypt? (See Exodus 14:15 – 16, 21 – 22, 26 – 28.)

Why did Moses do this, and what did his staff and hand represent?

4.  While pursuing the Israelites, what did Egyptian soldiers learn about the nature of the battle in which they were involved? (See Exodus 14:24 – 25.)

How correct was their assessment? (See Exodus 14:13 – 14.)

## Reflection

At the Red Sea, God demonstrated his sovereign power against Pharaoh and the gods of Egypt for the last time. Even though the Egyptians had treated his people harshly, God clearly desired for the Egyptians to know him and become partners with him in his story. Yet, in this final confrontation, Exodus 14:26 – 31 records the utter destruction of Pharaoh's army. Perhaps God executed judgment against Pharaoh because Pharaoh kept siding with the Egyptian gods — Osiris, Amun Re, Horus, and others — and steadfastly refused to accept him as the one, true, all-powerful, Creator God.

Once people are committed to an unbiblical worldview, why does it sometimes require a miracle of the Spirit of God to break through their ungodly thinking and lifestyle?

Think of how strong ungodly thinking or behavior can be in your own life. What has God had to do to get your attention so that you will change direction and choose shalom rather than chaos?

To what extent does God still desire all people — even those who may seem to be hopelessly steeped in chaos — to know him?

Think of how patient and compassionate God was in showing himself to Pharaoh and the Egyptians through the plagues, when he could have totally destroyed them at the beginning. What does his example say to you about the compassion and patience that we, as Christians today, should express toward people who don't know God and may even treat us badly?

Who in your life is steeped in chaos, and how do you think God might want you to "be God" to that person so that he or she may come to know his story?

God wanted his people to worship him for who he was, to recognize the life-giving, life-sustaining, life-changing nature of his kingdom, and participate fully with him in his unfolding story. Yet the gods of Egypt certainly had power and influence over God's people. How might Pharaoh's utter destruction in the sea, clearly a mighty act of God, have helped the Israelites leave Egypt's gods behind?

What in your life do you need to totally and completely leave behind — as if it has been destroyed in the sea by the hand of God — in order to join in fully with what God is doing today?

## Day Three | God's People Put Their Trust in Him

### The Very Words of God

*When the Israelites saw the great power the LORD displayed against the Egyptians, the people feared the LORD and put their trust in him and in Moses his servant.*

*Exodus 14:31*

## Bible Discovery

### *Leaving Egypt Behind*

When God began unfolding his plan to redeem his people from the physical and spiritual bondage of Egypt, he indicated that there were two parts to the process (Exodus 6:6 – 8). So that they would know he was their God, he first would bring them out of bondage; then he would make them his people and bring them into the Promised Land. The deliverance of his people through the Red Sea and the complete destruction of Pharaoh's army ended the confrontation between the God of the Hebrews and the gods of Egypt. For the Hebrews, Egypt was no more. Standing on the shore of the sea, they finally put their trust in their one, true, sovereign God. They also trusted in Moses, his chosen servant and their leader. Putting Egypt behind them, they faced a new life with the God who had redeemed them!

1.  As God began to act on behalf of his people, how did they respond, and what was the relationship between his acts of deliverance and their commitment to him? (See Exodus 4:29 – 31; 12:21 – 28; 14:16 – 31.)

2.  As God's plan for his people became known through his powerful actions on their behalf, how did the Hebrews' view of Moses change? (See Exodus 5:19 – 21; 14:31.)

    Do you think this change was necessary in order for God to accomplish his work in and through his people? Why or why not?

What does the Hebrews' thinking about Moses reveal to you about trusting and being faithful to a godly leader?

In consideration of how important the people's trust in Moses was, how great is the responsibility of leaders of God's people today to live a life of faithful obedience to God?

3.  Pharaoh led with a stick and dominating, harsh treatment. In contrast, what kind of treatment had the Israelites recognized in the way God led them? (See Exodus 15:13.)

What does this indicate about the type of leadership God expects from those who lead the flock on his behalf?

NOTE: The Hebrew word translated "guide," *nahal*, means "to lead a flock to a restful watering place."

4.  The crossing of the Red Sea was a pivotal event in the history of God's people. What do Joshua 4:20 – 24, Isaiah 51:9 – 10, and Isaiah 63:11 – 14 emphasize about that event?

Why do you think the Egyptians are not even mentioned?

## FOR GREATER UNDERSTANDING

### What Did It Mean for the Israelites to Put Their Trust in God?

When people today, Christian or not, talk about their relationship with deity, the expression "I believe in God" (or "I believe in a god") is often used. In ancient times, however, there was no sense of "believing in" a god. After they had seen the plagues and experienced the amazing events at the Red Sea, the question for the Israelites wasn't "Do you believe in God?" Of course they believed in God! It was obvious that God was real. The question was, did they trust him?

For the Israelites to put their *trust* in God and Moses also meant something different to them than it generally does for people today. The Hebrew understanding of *faith* and *trust* was not merely assent or commitment to a doctrine or creed. To put one's trust or faith in God always involved action, and the action of trust was expressed through obedience and commitment. So to have faith was to believe, trust, and act accordingly.

5.   Many Bible passages add to our understanding of trust and what it means to live a life of faith. As you read each of the following, write out the actions of faith — what it meant to put one's trust in God and obey him.

| The Text | The Actions of Faith, a Commitment to Obedience |
|---|---|
| Hab. 2:4 | |
| Gal. 3:11 | |
| Heb. 10:38–39 | |

| James 2:21–26 | |
|---|---|
| Heb. 11:1–38 | |

## Reflection

In today's world, it is far too easy for Christians to make mental commitments to God and yet not know him as he desires to be known and not trust him fully in response to his redemptive acts. As you consider what trust in God meant for the Israelites and what it means in your world, allow the perspective of Psalm 9:10 to guide your thinking: "Those who know your name will trust in you, for you, LORD, have never forsaken those who seek you."

On what is *your* faith and trust in God based, and in what way(s) has it deepened because of what you have seen God do?

How deeply rooted is your faith and trust in God and his Word as evidenced by your thoughts and actions toward him? As evidenced by your thoughts and actions toward other people? As evidenced by your career, hobbies, and/or pursuits?

In which area(s) of your life is there a "disconnect" between what you believe intellectually and your walk of faith (meaning your actions and faithful obedience to God)?

Who has God used, in your life or the life of a loved one, as a "Moses," an instrument of God's word and action?

How much trust did you place in that person, and how much did your trust in God depend on how that person lived?

Why is it vitally important for leaders of God's community to remain intensely faithful to him?

## Memorize

*And when the Israelites saw the great power the Lᴏʀᴅ displayed against the Egyptians, the people feared the Lᴏʀᴅ and put their trust in him and in Moses his servant.*

*Exodus 14:31*

# Day Four | The Israelites Sing a Hymn of Praise

## The Very Words of God

*The Lᴏʀᴅ is my strength and my song; he has become my salvation. He is my God, and I will praise him, my father's God, and I will exalt him.*

*Exodus 15:2*

## Bible Discovery

### *Joyfully Singing of the Greatness of God*

Commonly called the "Song of the Sea" (in Hebrew, *Shirat ha Yam*) by Jewish people and the "Song of Moses [and Miriam]" by Christians, the poetic song of Exodus 15 was clearly written by and for people who knew the Hebrews' history. The power of its words and beauty of its composition are enhanced when we know its historical and physical setting.

The song emphasizes God's love and protection for his people, his absolute sovereignty over nature, his greatness over all other gods, and his complete control of history in order to accomplish his purposes. It celebrates God's rescue of his people by the miraculous dividing of the sea as the paradigm of their salvation. It calls all people (and even creation itself) to see the works of the Lord and to give glory to him alone.

1.  Before you read this song (Exodus 15:1 – 18, 21), review in your mind the story leading up to the Israelites' dancing and singing on the shore of the sea. Keep in mind the events of Exodus 1 – 14 and read the song aloud several times. Imagine

yourself hearing it for the first time by the sea. Let its message and majesty speak to you. Offer it as an expression of praise and thanksgiving to your God.

a.   What was your first reaction to the song, and how did your response to it change as you read it several times?

**THE EASTERN SHORE OF THE PORTION OF THE RED SEA KNOWN TODAY AS THE GULF OF SUEZ. IT IS HIGHLY UNLIKELY THAT THE HEBREWS CROSSED EXACTLY HERE, BUT NOTICE THE TYPICAL SHORELINE AND SEVERE WILDERNESS ALL ALONG THE COAST. THE WIDE-OPEN BEACH SUGGESTS THE TYPE OF PLACE WHERE THE ISRAELITES DANCED AND SANG THE "SONG OF THE SEA."**

b.   Now take a closer look at the song. Which theme(s) are emphasized in the various portions of the song (see chart next page)? Why would each theme be important to the Israelites and their ongoing journey with God? Why would praising God for each theme be important for their relationship with him? In what ways would each theme be a testimony for future generations and for other people of God's greatness?

| Exodus 15 Text | Theme(s), Message, and Significance |
|---|---|
| vv. 1–10 (Moses) | |
| vv. 11–13 (Moses) | |
| vv. 14–16 (Moses) | |
| vv. 17–18 (Moses) | |
| v. 21 (Miriam) | |

## POINT TO PONDER
### Prepared to Praise?

When and where did the Israelites sing the "Song of the Sea" to the Lord? The word "then" in Exodus 15:1 indicates that the same miraculous event—Israel's safe crossing of the Red Sea and the destruction of Pharaoh's army in the sea—immediately preceded both the "Song of Moses" (Exodus 15:1–18) and the "Song of Miriam" (15:21). It is also likely that the Hebrews sang both parts of this song—consecutively or antiphonally—as part of one celebration of God's power and protecting love.

Try to picture the scene: thousands of Hebrews, young and old, joyfully and spontaneously singing and dancing on the shore of the sea. The women, tambourines in hand, sang and danced before the Lord. Perhaps others swayed and clapped in rhythm as wide-eyed children watched their elders express the joy of the Lord. These were exciting, life-changing moments in the history of God's people! They had seen God work in awesome power, and they broke out in unstoppable praise. Even today, observant Jews recite this song of praise and remembrance daily during morning prayer, weekly in synagogues, and yearly during the Passover.

Think about something for a moment. If you, like the Hebrews, had several hours to pack before leaving forever the only country you had known as home and walking across more than one hundred miles of desert, what would you take with you? Remember, you would have to carry virtually everything on your back. Would you have packed your tambourine, as many Hebrew women evidently did? (See Exodus 15:20.) Could it be that they already had anticipated times of dancing and celebration because their God was with them? Are you prepared to celebrate as you follow God where he leads in your life?

2. Exodus 15:13 reads, "In your unfailing love you will lead the people you have redeemed." No doubt this refers back to Exodus 6:6, where God promised to redeem his people. After the redemption of Israel from Egypt, the theme of redemption echoes throughout Scripture.

   a. Why was the exodus redemption experience so important for future generations in terms of providing a foundation for their identity, lifestyle, purpose, and hope? (See Deuteronomy 7:8 – 9; 13:1 – 5; 15:12 – 15; 24:17 – 18; 2 Samuel 7:22 – 24; Psalm 106:1 – 2, 7 – 12; Isaiah 44:21 – 23.)

b.  What is the role of Jesus the Messiah in God's redemption story? (See Galatians 3:13 – 14; 1 Peter 1:18 – 21.)

c.  What is your response to God's unfailing love as you see the thread of his redemption story woven throughout the Bible?

3.  The Israelites' spontaneous outpouring of praise after the crossing of the Red Sea became a model of praise for future followers of God. What connections do you see between the following passages and the Israelites' praises after their experience of God's redemption? (See 1 Chronicles 13:5 – 8; Psalm 102:18; 106:1; 149:1 – 4; 150.)

## THINK ABOUT IT

### Songs of Praise in the Ancient World

During the New Kingdom era of Egypt, which is the exodus time frame according to nearly every theory, ancient Egyptians customarily composed praise songs celebrating Pharaoh's great, heroic, and often superhuman exploits. Scholars have located such songs, including those on the stele honoring Merneptah and those honoring Ramses for his "great" victory over the Hittites. According to these songs, no one can compare in power, wisdom, and glory to Pharaoh. The "Song of the Sea" is a similar type of praise song in that it followed a great victory and focused on God alone as the object of praise.

These ancient songs honored the object of the praise and inspired those who sang and heard them. Jewish people today believe that their praise of God leads to him being recognized and praised by people who do not necessarily follow him. An example of this would be how Moses' praise of God and his great redemptive acts led his father-in-law, Jethro, to "enthrone" God by affirming that he was indeed the greatest of all the gods (Exodus 18:7 – 11).

The Merneptah Stele is a large, black granite pillar erected by Pharaoh Amenhotep III, and later inscribed by Merneptah who ruled from 1213 to 1203 BC. This stele commemorates a victory over the Libyans, but mentions a military campaign in Canaan in which Merneptah states that he defeated Ashkelon, Gezer, Yanoam, Israel, and others.

**THE MERNEPTAH STELE**

This stele, the only Egyptian reference to "Israel," is the earliest known reference to God's people outside the Bible. Many scholars refer to it as the "Israel Stele" although it only has one line about Israel. It is ironic to note that the translation of that line is: "Israel is laid waste, its seed no longer exists!" Many contemporary Jews find it humorous that the only reference to God's people outside the Bible is their obituary.

## Reflection

The "Song of the Sea" did more than capture the Hebrews' joy in their Creator God and what he had done for and through them during the exodus. This song provided a lasting interpretation of the exodus events they had experienced so that other people — Israelites as well as pagans — could recognize God and what he did and is doing in his world to defeat chaos! The "Song of the Sea" not only recognized God's hand in exodus events but explained why he did it, using the joy-filled, formerly enslaved Israelites as his instruments. This song gave God the glory and praise so that his reputation would precede Israel and be known among the nations.

What caused such a spontaneous celebration of joy and worship among the Israelites after they crossed the sea?

In contrast, why do you think so many of God's people today seem to find so little to celebrate?

How do you respond when you experience God's marvelous power, never-failing love, and undeserved deliverance?

In what way(s) are you "singing the 'Song of the Sea'" for other people, praising God so that they can know him and invite him to reign in their lives?

Why might we, the community of Jesus, need more "Miriams" to lead us in celebrating and praising the great God we worship?

What might we do to better recognize the times when we can physically demonstrate our deep love and commitment to God?

How might our lives and our world be different if we each "carried a tambourine" in expectation of God's awesome work in our lives?

Why is it important for us to celebrate the hand of God in our lives, honor and praise him, and identify and interpret his work for ourselves and for others?

## Memorize

*The Lord is my strength and my song; he has become my salvation.
He is my God, and I will praise him, my father's God, and I will exalt
him.*

*Exodus 15:2a*

or

*The Lord is my strength and my song; he has become my Yeshua [Jesus].
He is my God, and I will become a dwelling place for him, my father's
God, and I will exalt him.*

*Exodus 15:2b*

## THINK ABOUT IT

### Insights into the "Song of the Sea"

- *The LORD is my strength and my song.* The word translated "LORD" is *Jah*—the abbreviation of God's sacred name, *Jahweh*, which sets him apart from all other gods. The Hebrew word translated "song," *zimrat*, can also mean "defense." One Jewish midrash says that singing a song of praise to God results in God giving strength to the people who sing it.

- *He has become my salvation.* The Hebrew word translated "salvation" is *Yeshua*—the Hebrew way to say *Jesus*, the name his parents and disciples called him! Is this a hint from God, who saved the Israelites from Egypt as part of his unfolding plan to bring Jesus to provide the fullness of God's salvation through his death and resurrection?

- *He is my God.* This implies a rejection of Egypt's gods, and is an affirmation that the Hebrews will worship only *Jah*, not any other gods they may have worshiped previously (Joshua 24:14; Ezekiel 20:6–8). This can also be translated, "*This* is my God."

- *I will praise him.* The Hebrew word translated "praise" or "glorify," *an'veihu*, also comes from the root word *naveh*, meaning "oasis," a quiet, peaceful dwelling place. The Jewish Publication Society Torah translation reads: "I will enshrine him," meaning, "I will be a house for him." Consider this in light of Exodus 19:4 and 25:8, which stated that God's purpose in redeeming Israel is to bring them to himself and to live among them!

  Was Moses, as some Jewish scholars believe, teaching Israel that they were to be a temple of God's presence to the world? God wanted his nation to be the holy place where his presence dwelled. So in that sense they were to become his temple for the world as well as becoming his priests (Exodus 19:5–6). Notice where God's presence dwelled during Hebrew Bible times (2 Chronicles 6:1–3; 7:1–3) and Jesus' time (Matthew 23:20–21; Acts 2:1–4; Romans 8:9–11; 1 Corinthians 3:16–17). Where does God dwell today? (See 1 Peter 2:4–5.)

  NOTE: For further study on God's dwelling place, please refer to the lessons in *That the World May Know* Set 4, session 9, "Power to the People," and Set 6, session 3, "The Presence of God—A Countercultural Community."

# **Day Five** | When the Lord Reigns

## The Very Words of God

> *"Now if you obey me fully and keep my covenant, then out of all nations you will be my treasured possession. Although the whole earth is mine, you will be for me a kingdom of priests and a holy nation." These are the words you are to speak to the Israelites.*

> **Exodus 19:5 – 6**

## Bible Discovery

### *God's Kingdom Comes as We Obey His Will*

Despite the Israelites' commitment to God's reign, evidenced in the "Song of the Sea," they were not yet ready to bring knowledge of him to the whole world. As proclaimed in the exodus, the reign of God (later to be called the kingdom of God, or kingdom of heaven) comprises three elements:

- The kingdom begins with the power of God in action — God's "finger" (Exodus 8:16 – 19).

- Those who recognize his power and acknowledge his reign call him *Lord* (Exodus 15:18).

- Those who call him Lord obey him so that his kingdom will advance as his will is done (Exodus 19:3 – 6).

What did the Israelites need to do and receive in order for God's reign over their lives to be complete? In response to God's deliverance, having made a commitment of faith, they had to learn to obey God so that his kingdom would advance as his will was done.

1. Because of what God had done for the Israelites in his grace, and as a response to their confession that he was their Lord (King) who reigned over them, what did he command of

them so they would become a part of his reign — a "kingdom of priests and a holy nation"? (See Exodus 19:1 - 6.)

2.  Before God gave his people the Ten Commandments to be obeyed, he summarized his great and gracious act of redemptive deliverance from Egypt. What is the basis for God calling his people to obedience? (See Exodus 20:1 - 2.)

Why did his act of gracious redemption demand the response of obedience?

Why do you think God gave the Ten Commandments *after* the redemption from Egypt, the crossing of the Red Sea, and the Israelites' journey to Mount Sinai instead of at the *beginning* of Exodus or Genesis?

3.  We can gain further insights into the Jewish understanding of the kingdom of God by moving forward and studying Jesus' teaching. Just as his teaching and life adds to and broadens our understanding of the kingdom of God, the Jewish context deepens our understanding of his teaching. As

you read the following portions of the Christian text, write down the themes of their teaching in relationship to the kingdom of God (kingdom of heaven).

| Bible Text | Person(s) Involved | Theme Emphasized |
|---|---|---|
| Matt. 3:1–3 | John the Baptizer | |
| Matt. 4:17, 23; 5:10; 6:33; 9:35–38; Luke 4:43; 8:1–2; Acts 1:1–3 | Jesus | |
| Matt. 10:5–8; 24:14; Luke 9:1–2 | Jesus and his disciples | |
| Acts 8:12 | Philip | |
| Acts 19:8 | Paul | |

## DID YOU KNOW?

There is no more central theme in Jesus' teaching than the kingdom of God (the kingdom of heaven). The Christian church has understood the kingdom of God (kingdom of heaven) in many different ways. It has been understood as the place believers go after death. It has been identified with a coming "Messianic Age" or as actually being the same as the institutional church. Some people have made a distinction between the kingdom of God and the kingdom of heaven. It would be well worth your time to study all of Jesus' teachings on the kingdom of God in order to comprehend it in all of its richness. Whenever Jesus taught about the kingdom of God that he came to bring, it seems that its infant beginnings are rooted in the story of the exodus.[1]

4.  What similarities do you recognize between what is happening in Exodus 8:19 and Luke 11:14 – 20? (Hint: Focus on how Jesus described his power and the effect of that power on demonic powers and other people.)

## POINT TO PONDER

When we pray, "Your kingdom come" (Matthew 6:10), we are not simply praying for Jesus to return soon to finish his work, although that request is biblically sound. This phrase is also a prayer that God's reign will be more and more evident in our lives and in the aspects of his world for which we have responsibility. The phrase "your will be done" is a Hebrew parallelism meaning, "May your kingdom come as your will is done." So it is a prayer for God's grace that also demands our acts of faith.

**FROM THE SHORE OF THE RED SEA, THE ISRAELITES HEADED INLAND, WHERE GOD CONTINUED THEIR TRAINING IN OBEDIENCE SO THAT HIS WILL WOULD BE DONE — A DISCIPLINE CHRISTIANS TODAY MUST EXPERIENCE AS WELL.**

5.  Why wasn't it enough for the ancient Hebrews to celebrate God's reign as Lord (Exodus 15:1 – 3) and for people of Jesus' day just to say, "Lord, Lord" (Matthew 7:21 – 23)? How did God expect people who called him *Lord* and received his salvation to respond? (See Exodus 12:24; 19:5; John 14:15, 23 – 24.)

## Reflection

God redeems in order to rule the redeemed, and through the obedience of the redeemed a part of his creation is restored to him. So, just as the Israelites had to choose whether or not to respond to the evidence of God's kingdom as shown through the power of God's "finger" and acknowledge him as their reigning Lord, we have that choice. When we respond as the Israelites did beside the Red Sea, there is a sense in which their song becomes our song. When the freed Israelites danced and sang praises to their God who had redeemed them and who reigned over them, however, their journey had just begun. They were not yet the people God desired them to be. Did they understand what they had been freed from enough to demonstrate their grateful devotion by obeying him? Would they advance the kingdom and take up their place in God's story by their obedience? These are the same questions we must ask ourselves.

Jesus has brought the saving power of God's kingdom to us. Everyone who acknowledges God as King may enter into it. But Jesus also said, "If anyone loves me, he will obey my teaching. My Father will love him, and we will come to him and make our home with him" (John 14:23).

Do you think that God coming to make his home with you, so that his presence will dwell in your life, is part of what it means to be a part of the kingdom of God? Why or why not?

What do you think a person must do in order to *experience* the kingdom of heaven?

To what extent have you experienced this kingdom?

What impact do you think Christians who seem to lack a passion to obey God in everything and who live a less-than-godly life-style have on: other followers of Jesus? people who do not know God? the advancement of God's kingdom?

To what extent do other people see God's reign by your obedience to his commands?

To what extent have you brought God's kingdom into reality in your community or family by:

Experiencing and acknowledging his saving power — his "finger"?

Calling him "Lord" and inviting him to reign in your life?

Bringing some aspect of his world under his reign by your obedience to his commands?

## Memorize

*Not everyone who says to me, "Lord, Lord," will enter the kingdom of heaven, but only he who does the will of my Father who is in heaven.*

**Matthew 7:21**

# NOTES

## Introduction

1. Jesus' death (as the Lamb of God) was apparently on Passover; he was buried as the Unleavened Bread festival began, and was raised at the beginning of First Fruit.

2. Since I hold the Bible to be God's revealed word, I reject the arguments of many scholars who do not believe the exodus occurred or at least did not occur as the Bible describes it.

3. A defense of this position can be found in *The Moody Atlas of Bible Lands* by Barry J. Beitzel (Chicago: Moody Press, 1985).

4. A defense of this position can be found in *Exploring Exodus: The Origins of Biblical Israel* by Nahum M. Sarna (New York: Schocken Books, 1996).

## Session Three

1. This perspective on the ten plagues is based on the research of Ziony Zevit, as published in the article "Three Ways to Look at the Ten Plagues" (*Bible Review,* June 1990). While I do not share all of his perspectives, I find his understanding of the plagues as based on the creation account to be extremely helpful.

## Session Four

1. I am indebted to G. K. Beale's in-depth study of the issue of Pharaoh's heart and its connection to Paul's discussion of the hardening of hearts in the book of Romans. The article, "An Exegetical and Theological Consideration of the Hardening of Pharaoh's Heart in Exodus 4 – 14 and Romans 9," is an excellent, textually based exploration of a complex issue. (See *Trinity Journal* 5 NS [1984]: 129 – 154.)

## Session Five

1. Dwight Pryor's work, *Unveiling the Kingdom of Heaven* (Center for Judaic-Christian Studies), is a helpful review of Jesus' understanding of the kingdom of God.

# BIBLIOGRAPHY

To learn more about the cultural and geographical background of the Bible, please consult the following resources.

Beale, G. K. "An Exegetical and Theological Consideration of the Hardening of Pharaoh's Heart in Exodus 4–14 and Romans 9." *Trinity Journal* 5 NS, 1984, pages 129–154.

Beitzel, Barry J. *The Moody Atlas of Bible Lands.* Chicago: Moody Press, 1985.

Bottéro, Jean, Elana Cassin and Jean Vercoutter, eds. *Near East: The Early Civilizations.* New York: Delacorte Press, 1967.

Davis, John J. *Moses and the Gods of Egypt: Studies in the Book of Exodus.* Grand Rapids, Mich.: Baker Book House, 1971.

Edersheim, Alfred. *The Temple: Its Ministry and Services as They Were at the Time of Jesus Christ.* London: James Clarke & Co., 1959.

———. *The Life and Times of Jesus the Messiah.* Peabody, Mass.: Hendrickson Publishers, 1993.

Feiler, Bruce. *Walking the Bible: A Journey by Land through the Five Books of Moses.* New York: HarperCollins, 2002.

Fretheim, Terrence E. *Exodus: Interpretation, A Bible Commentary for Teaching and Preaching.* Louisville: John Knox Press, 1991.

Friedman, Richard Elliott. *Commentary on the Torah.* San Francisco: Harper, 2001.

Hoffmeier, James K. *Ancient Israel in Sinai.* Oxford: Oxford University Press, 2005.

———. *Israel in Egypt.* Oxford: Oxford University Press, 1997.

Lesko, Barbara and Leonard. "Pharaoh's Workers." *Biblical Archaeology Review.* January/February 1999.

Lesko, Leonard H., ed. *Pharaoh's Workers.* Ithaca, N.Y.: Cornell University Press, 1994.

Levenson, Jon D. *Sinai and Zion: An Entry into the Jewish Bible.* San Francisco: Harper, 1985.

Levine, Baruch A. *The JPS Torah Commentary: Leviticus*. Philadelphia: Jewish Publication Society, 1990.

Milgrom, Jacob. *The JPS Torah Commentary: Numbers*. Philadelphia: Jewish Publication Society, 1991.

Peterson, Eugene. *Eat This Book*. Grand Rapids, Mich.: Eerdmans Publishing, 2006.

Pryor, Dwight. *Unveiling the Kingdom of Heaven*. Dayton, Ohio: Center for Judaic Christian Studies, 2008.

Sarna, Nahum. *The JPS Torah Commentary: Exodus*. Philadelphia: Jewish Publication Society, 1991.

———. *The JPS Torah Commentary: Genesis*. Philadelphia: Jewish Publication Society, 1989.

———. *Exploring Exodus: The Origins of Biblical Israel*. New York: Schocken Books, 1996.

Silverman, David P. *Ancient Egypt*. Oxford: Oxford University Press, 1997.

Tigay, Jeffrey H. *The JPS Torah Commentary: Deuteronomy*. Philadelphia: Jewish Publication Society, 1996.

Watterson, Barbara. *Gods of Ancient Egypt*. London: Sutton Publishing, 1996.

Wilkinson, Richard H. *The Complete Gods and Goddesses of Ancient Egypt*. New York: Thames and Hudson, 2003.

———. *The Complete Temples of Ancient Egypt*. New York: Thames and Hudson, 2000.

Zevit, Ziony. "Three Ways to Look at the Ten Plagues." *Bible Review,* June 1990.

# WEBSITE RESOURCES

## Related to the temple of Amun Re at Karnak, Egypt:

*http://touregypt.net/featurestories/templeofamun.htm*

Article by Jimmy Dunn (includes reference sources) provides an overview of the temple of Amun Re at Karnak.

*www.touregypt.net/featurestories/karnak2.htm*

Several articles by Jim Fox (which include reference sources) about the different parts of the temple of Amun Re.

*www.eyelid.co.uk/karnakb.htm*

Provides an interactive map of the temple with photos.

*http://dlib.etc.ucla.edu/projects/Karnak*

A very good source that includes timelines and digital representations of the Karnak temple complex from different angles and periods.

*http://en.wikipedia.org/wiki/karnak*

Overview of the Karnak temple complex and information about the precinct of Amun Re. (CAVEAT: Wikipedia allows ANYONE to contribute information. It should therefore be scrutinized against other reliable sources for accuracy.)

*www.ancient-wisdom.co.uk/egyptkarnak.htm*

General information about Karnak and pictures of the main temple complex.

*www.bibleplaces.com/karnak.htm*

Pictures and an overview of the Karnak temple complex and a list of related websites.

*www.pbs.org/wgbh/nova/egypt/explore/karnakrams.html*

Interesting site with 360-degree interactive cameras positioned inside the temple of Amun Re.

## Related to the pyramids of Egypt:

*www.guarduans.net/egypt/pyramids.htm*
Extensive collection of websites dedicated to the pyramids of Egypt.

*http://en.wikipedia.org/wiki/Egyptian_pyramids*
General information on the history, symbolism, and locations of pyramids with further readings and external links. (CAVEAT: Wikipedia allows ANYONE to contribute information. It should therefore be scrutinized against other reliable sources for accuracy.)

*www.pbs.org/wgbh/nova/pyramid*
Website related to the NOVA documentary "This Old Pyramid." Useful information on construction of the pyramids and the attempt to reconstruct a pyramid.

*www.bbc.co.uk/history/ancient/egyptians/great_pyramid_01.shtml*
Loaded with scholarly articles, interactive content, timelines, etc.

*www.eyelid.co.uk/pyr-temp.htm*
Information on pyramids and temples, including computer generated reconstructions, interactive ground maps, photos, paintings and drawings.

*www.egyptologyonline.com/welcome.htm*
Provides information, resources, and scholarly articles on a variety of topics related to Egyptology.

*www.ancientegypt.co.uk/pyramids/home.html*
The British Museum educational website on ancient Egypt. Includes stories showing the building of the pyramids and interactive exploration of a pyramid.

*www.nationalgeographic.com/pyramids/pyramids.html*
Website related to National Geographic's documentary "Egypt: Secrets of the Ancient World." Includes interactive timelines of ancient Egypt and the pyramids.

*ww.bibleplaces.com/giza.htm*
Pictures and brief information about the pyramids of Giza. Includes a list of related websites.

*ww.touregypt.net/featurestories/pyramids.htm*
Features extensive scholarly articles about ancient Egypt and the pyramids.